The

ULTIMATE MEAL PREP GUIDE TO

SIMPLIFY
CLEAN
EATING

The
ULTIMATE MEAL PREP GUIDE TO
SIMPLIFY
CLEAN
EATING

HOW TO COOK
ONCE TO
SAVE MONEY &
FEEL BETTER
...IN JUST 4 HOURS
A MONTH

Wendy Massey, RN, BHS

Cover Design: Tehsin Gul
Interior: Amit Dey
Photo credit: Christopher Carroll

ISBN: 9798386206673

DEDICATION

To my son, Matthew, who helped transform me from an angry, protective "momma bear" to one who joined you in accepting your health conditions were gifts to be used for God's glory.

To my daughter, Kirstie, Massey Wellness, LLC would not be able to stay afloat without you. You are my voice of reason, my calm in the storms, and my millennial genius who can find a way to simplify what I try to make so difficult.

To my husband, Bill, who has loved me and appreciated all of my kitchen experiments, sinks of dishes, and piles of laundry that you have taken over during my many long days and nights of completing this book while still working so hard to help people get well.

And most importantly, to Jesus Christ, my Lord, and Savior. I am so undeserving of the rich blessings You have provided me, and I am so incredibly grateful for this burden You've placed in my heart of a message that must spread far and wide to help heal Your Kingdom. I can do none of this without You, and You get all of the glory!

FOREWORD

As someone who has a deep passion for health in all areas of life; physically, emotionally, and spiritually, I was immediately drawn to the practicality and beautiful collection of recipes, tips, and scripture woven throughout. One of the key factors in preventing and overcoming any illness and disease is what we eat. Whether you are a new on your journey to health, a long-time health advocate, work inside or outside of the home, this book will help you invest in your future and those you love.

Gone are the days of bland, boring meals and wasted ingredients. With this book, you'll have access to healthy and flavorful meals. It is a must-have for anyone who wants to take control of their health and wellness through food.

Wendy provides an easy roadmap to follow and debunks the myths that a healthy lifestyle is too expensive, too cumbersome, too time consuming, and tasteless. By being mindful of what we eat and serve our families, we can honor the Lord and fulfill our responsibility to care for the bodies He has given us.

Get ready to say goodbye to mealtime stress and hello to delicious and nutritious meals with this amazing meal prep strategy book.

Ivelisse Page
Executive Director & Co-Founder, BelieveBig.org

TABLE OF CONTENTS

A GIFT FOR YOU

Friend, you will read references to so many delicious foods throughout this book that are some of my favorite Meal Prep recipes. I have included 50 of them in an eCookbook that I want you to have for free! My eCookbooks are for sale on my website, but I am giving you this token of my appreciation because you have taken the time to read this and go through this journey with me! It means the world!

Now, as you're reading along and see the title of something that sounds mouthwatering, I've likely included it in this eCookbook, especially for you!

Not only will you get these recipes, but everyone who snags this collection of recipes will also get "Massey's Monday Meal" delivered to your inbox early every Monday morning! This weekly message is a favorite among my wellness circle, as it inspires you with new healthy, delicious recipes you and your family will love!

Just visit Gift.SimplifyCleanEating.com or scan this QR code to get your copy right away:

INTRODUCTION AND IMPACT

Don't you realize that all of you together are the temple of God and that the Spirit of God lives in you? God will destroy anyone who destroys this temple. For God's temple is holy, and you are that temple.

1 Corinthians 3:16-17 NLT

I often hear it: "I don't have time to Meal Prep!" or "Eating healthy is too expensive!" You are not alone if you have ever said or thought those words. But I'm here to tell you, if you are a busy human, like most of us in the hustle and bustle of this spinning rock we live on, YOU do not have time NOT to Meal Prep! I'm also going to debunk the lies about eating healthy. Quite honestly, your health and your wallet depend on what I'm going to relay! Adopting a healthy lifestyle has never been more critical than it is right now.

Our world is falling victim to the disease of convenience. Every day, we are given entirely too many unhealthy choices, like pre-packaged and highly processed foods, quick fixes, fast food drive-thru options, delivery services, etc. These conveniences are killing us! Chronic diseases like diabetes, heart disease, obesity, cancer, a slew of autoimmune diseases, and so much more are all on the rise. Western medicine improves our symptoms and even increases our life span, but the reality is that *disease management* has improved, and we are living longer, sicker lives.

Sister, Christians are amongst the world's worst about healthy eating. We are God's temple, which is holy, as the opening verse reminds us. Yikes! Is that convicting or what?! How many have taken that charge seriously when we have pizza night at the church or Sunday morning doughnuts between services?

Before I completely lose you here and have you ready to throw this book across the room, I want you to consider this: It's not the once-in-a-while pizza and doughnuts that are the problem. We have become a culture dependent on a highly processed, highly convenient, high sugar, high carb, high starch, low nutritional value Standard American Diet. The result is a lack of energy and not sleeping, and we become increasingly ill over time. This deterioration usually happens slowly, without us even realizing it. Those who strive to be Proverbs 31 women are no longer "energetic and strong" (Proverbs 31:17) to complete the tasks God has given us while we are on this earth.

What is your mission while you're here if you are a Christian? We all have one! You could be charged with raising the most extraordinary family ever. Dear sister, you need to be strong for that task! You need the knowledge to feed them healthily to grow them into strong young men and women who are also ready to do God's will. If, as a collective Church (big C intended), we all continue to decline in health because we have fallen victim to convenience, who will be left to be strong enough to carry out God's mission on this earth?

While you may think your mission is small and confined within the walls of your home, I want you to hear what I am about to say and then REREAD it three times! You have no idea the level of impact you can have by raising your family of 2, 4, or 10 when you present them strong enough to be used by God for His mission. Imagine the cascade of goodwill when your family impacts others, and then others after them, others after them, and so on! That is IMPACT! And it can all start and change with you, how you care for yourself, your family, and their temple! Wow. That's huge!

Some of you may believe you have a larger, maybe even a massive mission from God. This is how I feel. I think this mission is a revolution - a movement to reach as many of God's children as possible and teach the importance, necessity, and ease of living a simplified, healthy lifestyle. Several years ago, I was a 65-pound heavier pre-diabetic who would get winded if I climbed a set of stairs, spiraling out of control with my carb cravings. That's right. I've been there. There was no way I could be up for the mission God had planned for me. I heard His call and began my transformation journey. You, too, can decide today that your current health, low energy level, weight, or whatever is stopping you from being up to the task God has called you to do will be a thing of the past.

I will tell you now that doing nothing is not an option. If you already eat clean and natural foods, you understand how life-changing this is. However, if you are addicted to the disease of convenience, you will become more ill rapidly and be less available to God, your family, your children, and your grandchildren. I hate to paint this dismal picture, but it is true.

I have great news, though! God has gifted me with the ability to educate and inspire others! After He helped heal me, He guided me through how to help others heal. You do not have to become less healthy! Today is the perfect time to start your transformation! If you adopt the principles I teach in this book, you will have a huge perspective change. You will learn just how much control you have over your health and how possible it is to live a simplified, clean, healthy lifestyle. It takes work, a mindset shift, and new skills, but I will guide you through every step! And age doesn't matter either! I have worked with clients in their 70s who now feel better and stronger than they did in their 30s.

I will teach you to fill your home with healthy meals for an entire month. I have developed a monthly meal prep strategy that can save the average American from 24 to 30 hours a month in the kitchen. Even if you are a novice cook, these strategies are simple and easy to do.

Do you still believe you don't have time to meal prep? I've been where you are. I was a 60-70 hour-a-week Emergency Department Registered Nurse and a single mom of two teenagers. I truly believed at the time that no one was busier than me. But, as you will read, I was forced into feeding my family healthily due to my son's sudden poor health. I had to learn how to accomplish as much as possible with as little time available and take charge of improving my family's health. With a bit of practice, the meal prep strategies you will learn in this book can be whittled down to just a few hours. Imagine a month's worth of meals in just a fraction of a day!

Feeding your family clean, natural, yummy foods while maintaining a busy life is not only possible but necessary! You and they will love the food, and I can't wait to guide you on your journey to this new lifestyle!

Just one last thought before you turn the page and dive in. This passage changed my life when I was whining about the lack of time to undergo this lifestyle change. King Solomon was harsh when he wrote this Proverb, but even I, the self-proclaimed least lazy person on earth, needed to hear it:

> Take a lesson from the ants, you lazybones. Learn from their ways and become wise! Though they have no prince or governor or ruler to make them work, they labor hard all summer, gathering food for the winter. But you, lazybones, how long will you sleep? When will you wake up? A little extra sleep, a little more slumber, a little folding of the hands to rest— then poverty will pounce on you like a bandit; scarcity will attack you like an armed robber.
>
> —Proverbs 6:6-11

I hope you feel it as much as I did when it first convicted me. Now, let's dive in.

Chapter 1

OUR MISSION

You say, "I am allowed to do anything"—but not everything is good for you. And even though "I am allowed to do anything," I must not become a slave to anything.

1 Corinthians 6:12

So, why do we need to be concerned with the health of our world? And is this a "new" problem? Let me start with some data to illustrate my concern.

Health is more than how you look in jeans, friend. Food corporations first introduced pre-packaged, highly processed foods in the 1950s. At that time, according to an article in the American Journal of Medicine, the obesity rate (>30 BMI) of men was 10.2%, with just 0.5% with a morbid obesity rate (>35 BMI). For women, it was 13.9%, with just 3.9% with a morbid obesity rate.[1] The CDC reported the obesity rate for all Americans in 2020 was 41.9%, with a morbid obesity rate of 9.2%.[2]

---

[1] Nisha I. Parikh, MD, MPH, Michael J. Pencina, PhD, Thomas J. Wang, MD, Katherine J. Lanier, BS, Caroline S. Fox, MD,Ralph B. D'Agostino, PhD, Ramachandran S. Vasan, MD, "Increasing Trends in Incidence of Overweight and Obesity over 5 Decades," The American Journal of Medicine, Vol 120, No 3, March 2007, https://www.amjmed.com/article/S0002-9343(06)00674-7/pdf.
[2] Centers for Disease Control and Prevention, "Adult Obesity Facts", CDC, (last review) May 12, 2022, https://www.cdc.gov/obesity/data/adult.html.

Let's look at the average from 1950s data and compare it to all adults in the recent data. These statistics demonstrate a 250% increase in obesity rate and over 315% in morbid obesity in just 70 years!

In the same period, the incidence of diabetes rose from 0.93% (1958) to 11.3% (2022).[3] This increase is more than 1100%! These rates are staggering! Diabetes causes kidney failure, blindness, worsening heart disease, and death. Also, according to the CDC, heart disease is the leading cause of death.[4] One person dies every 34 seconds from heart disease.

I could give you similar statistics for cancer and a host of autoimmune diseases, many of which didn't exist 30-40 years ago. One thing rings unanimously true for all reputable sources reporting on disease prevention: Diet and lifestyle are the top reasons for Americans' poor health.

The devil is at work in a big way, attacking us where he can. In this case, through our gluttony and laziness. But this is not your fault, sweet sister. The enemy is as cunning as can be! Many toxins and chemicals added to our foods are designed—YES, on purpose—to create an addictive taste and leave you unsatisfied, so you keep coming back for more! I will go into this in greater detail later in this book.

Rather than allowing all of this information to depress you completely, let me assure you that God can deliver us from our temptations! Scripture reminds us:

> The temptations in your life are no different from what others experience. And God is faithful. He will not allow the temptation to be more than you can stand. When you are tempted, he will show you a way out so that you can endure.
>
> —1 Corinthians 10:13

---

[3] Centers for Disease Control and Prevention, "National Diabetes Statistics Report", CDC, (last review) June 29, 2022, https://www.cdc.gov/diabetes/data/statistics-report/index.html.
[4] Centers for Disease Control and Prevention, "Heart Disease Facts", CDC, (last review) October 14, 2022, https://www.cdc.gov/heartdisease/facts.htm.

I am here to share that way out! So, let us move on to what we should do about it. Should we just accept that we are part of an increasingly ill world, or should we take control? Oh, wait, you didn't know you could take control? Let me tell you how God led me to this changed mindset.

I was a well-decorated Emergency and Trauma Registered Nurse for nearly two decades. When it came to conventional or "Western Medicine," I was all in! Then one day, I suddenly became the mom of a very sick young adult male. My 18-year-old son became a Type 1 Diabetic. About six months later, he began having a gastrointestinal disorder. For nine long months, we sought the answers to the causes of his new illness. Specialists were prescribing more and more pills and ordering more and more tests.

Meanwhile, my previously healthy, six-foot-tall son had dropped to 118 pounds. NOTHING was improving. In fact, he was getting sicker and sicker. The day we left Johns Hopkins after visiting the reportedly "top pediatric gastroenterologist this side of the Mississippi River," I WAS DONE. All he had accomplished was to prescribe my son an antidepressant. I knew my kid! I am not saying he wasn't depressed with his poor health at such a young age, understandably so, but I felt they were putting a bandaid on an underlying issue that NO ONE was figuring out!

A couple of weeks earlier, it dawned on me that none of these specialists had asked me what my kid was eating! NOT ONE! It was a GI issue, and no one thought diet could be a factor?! I began researching different foods and symptoms and felt prepared to test some things on him myself. When we were leaving Hopkins, having yet again been failed by "Western Medicine," I asked Matthew, "are you ready to take this on ourselves?" His answer broke my heart, but it motivated me. He said, "Momma, I'll do ANYTHING to feel better!" And he meant it.

We spent the next six weeks doing a total elimination diet and slowly added back potential trigger foods. We quickly discovered that my son was intolerant to gluten and processed foods. He also had mild reactions to multiple other foods, but gluten was his biggest trigger. In that short six weeks, my son was off all the prescription medications he had started over the previous nine months except insulin. He regained enough strength and energy in six weeks through his new clean food lifestyle to run a 10k event! At the time of this book, it has been nearly 12 years, and, I am happy to report, he is still healthy and has NEVER been hospitalized or put on additional medications for diabetes or what we now know as celiac disease.

This entire experience blew my mind. I suddenly realized that the world needed to know how much control individuals could have over their health just by eating the right food. I also learned that most medical schools do not educate doctors adequately in nutrition to bring one's diet into their evaluations. God's grace led me from a very negative, angry place to one where I realized it was not the doctors' fault. That awakening was when I realized my mission! My calling is to make a difference!

Over the years, I have worked with countless family members to improve their health. My sister had been misdiagnosed with fibromyalgia, and my husband battled rheumatoid arthritis. Later I also helped my husband through his cancer therapy as an adjunct to his chemotherapy and radiation. My daughter needed dietary assistance with PCOS, and several others close to us wanted me to teach them how to take control of their health through nutrition.

I've also worked with hundreds of clients since the inception of Massey Wellness. Every client who has put all my recommendations in place has improved their health. Many changes have been very drastic!

My Lifestyle Transformation program, which is fully nutrition-focused, has helped folks improve their health and reduce or eliminate the need for medications that control their lives. My clients have an improved mindset, increased energy, and vitality. As a bonus, the side effect of my transformation program is weight loss when needed! I've helped people of all ages who have had weight to gain, no weight to lose, and others lose over 100 pounds. Weight control is part of my diet and lifestyle, not the focus!

I also love how much this has extended to my clients' families. Spouses and children willing to follow along have also had tremendous improvements in their health! One of my absolute favorite quotes comes from my client and dear friend, Angi. When she was teaching her teenagers the importance of eating natural foods, she said, "Eating food from a box eventually leads to your body being in a box!" Morbid but effective! Luckily, her kids enjoyed the food, and it made everyone happy that they had more control over what was going into their bodies.

It is important to note that everything I teach, every class, book, webinar, etc., uses REAL FOOD. THERE ARE NO GIMMICKS that I recommend (i.e., diet pills, shakes, powders, bars, etc.). For this healthy lifestyle, you will only need real food that you can access in your grocery store, farmers market, or maybe an occasional online purchase. While occasional supplementation is helpful, I make it my mission to teach you how expensive additional "diet" products sold are unnecessary and often detrimental to your health.

Now that you understand my passion for health through natural nutrition - what does this have to do with Meal Prep? Meal Prep is an absolute NECESSITY to a healthy lifestyle in this busy world. Unless you are a rare gem who lives for spending every minute in the kitchen AND have time to do it, then you NEED to prepare meals ahead of time!

One of my favorite authors is the President of Proverbs 31 Ministries, Lysa Terkeurst. In her New York Times Bestselling Book "Made to Crave," she references 1 Corinthians 10:13. She states, "The way out The Lord provides for me is deciding in advance what I will and won't have each day."[5]

---

[5] Lysa Terkeurst. *Made To Crave: Satisfying Your Deepest Desire With God, Not Food.* Grand Rapids, Michigan: Zondervan, 2010, pg. 159

Most people fail in a healthy lifestyle because they don't do the legwork to ensure they have their home filled with healthy foods at all times. When I was preparing to write this book, my mentor, Donna Partow, felt led to a verse from God just before we met. "Lazy people don't even cook the game they catch, but the diligent make use of everything they find" (Proverbs 12:27). Once I shared my mission with her, she was confident I was the reason God laid that verse on her.

So let's be diligent, my friend. We must be strong enough for whatever task God calls us, or the Church will continue to weaken. He may not *need* us, but He *wants* to use His children in His work on this earth. What I am about to ask you to do may seem overwhelming. Still, please let me assure you that I have developed quite a system that will equip you with every-thing you need to accomplish a once-a-month meal prep strategy that will become a time-saver, a money saver, AND a health saver.

All I ask is your willingness to listen and learn. Set aside any preconceived notions you have about a healthy lifestyle. I have heard it all," too hard," "too expensive," "food tastes like cardboard," "too time-consuming," "too restrictive,"—set it aside. Or maybe you are like who I was before I learned better. I was a yo-yo dieter who yo-yoed my way right into a poor metabo-lism and THOUGHT I knew about healthy eating. After three weeks of nutrition classroom training in nursing school, I was adequately educated, after all. (Insert eye roll.) Set it all aside, and consider what I will teach you throughout the rest of this book.

My hope and prayer are that you, too, will have the "awakening" of just how amazing it is that God provides us with all of the perfect foods on this earth naturally. They taste better and will make you feel so much better than any pre-packaged manufactured foods. I pray that you will learn to be as angry (or at least concerned), as I am, that the majority of foods sold on our gro-cery store shelves are full of poison, causing an epidemic of obesity and disease. I also pray that you will go all in and realize just how much better and energetic you feel and that you share this with your family.

With all of this new knowledge, you will be prepared and capable of whatever you are called to do. Be bold and share this with the world. People do not know this stuff! We need a revolution in massive proportions! The effect of processed foods is a generational epidemic, and most of us alive today do not remember a life without convenience foods. The world needs to be educated and healed! Dramatic? It seems so—until you are the one who has been dramatically healed.

Let's get to work!

Chapter 2

R.I.C.H.E.S.

Beloved, I pray that in all respects you may prosper and be in good health, just as your soul prospers.

3 John 1:2 NASB

A lright! I'm so glad I have not scared you off! Let's talk about R.I.C.H.E.S! Wait, what? Are you confused because you thought you purchased a book about meal prep and eating healthy, not finances? You did! Just wait!

What I will teach you will make you rich in health, save you money, AND save you time. We are talking about a different kind of R.I.C.H.E.S.

Let me explain the acronym I use to guide you into this amazing life of healthy meal prep.

R — Realization
I — Inventory/Identify
C — Calendar
H — Harvest
E — Execute
S — Storage

R.I.C.H.E.S. is the acronym I felt led to as I developed my Monthly Meal Prep strategy, and I thought it was poignant. You may find it interesting that the word "prosper" in the opening scripture reference of this chapter was translated from the Greek verb "euodoō," literally meaning to "have a good road," i.e., have an easy successful path ahead of you. Looking more deeply into this word sheds much light on my prayer for you as you embark on this new journey and lifestyle. I want you to prosper in health, have a good road, and follow the R.I.C.H.E.S.

Allow me to illustrate how you will save time with this strategy. According to a New York Post article,[6] in research conducted by One Poll, the average American spends approximately 67 minutes a day in their kitchen, which equates to over 400 hours yearly! But since we're talking about a new practice to adopt monthly, let me give you an example of how meal prepping saves time per month. I spend four hours each month on my Monthly meal Prep strategy. Outside of that one day, I spend an average of 10 minutes a day in the kitchen now, and that average may be high. Most days, it takes 30 seconds to put a meal in a slow cooker and go back in and scoop it into a bowl. Some days, it's simply heating premade chili in the microwave. So when I tell you an average of 10 minutes, I'm being generous. Therefore, if I average 10 minutes in the kitchen daily, that's 300 minutes or 5 hours. Add that to my Monthly Meal Prep of 4 hours, and I've spent nine whopping hours in the kitchen for the month!

With the One Poll average of 67 minutes, that's 33.5 hours each month in the kitchen! I just gave you back 24 hours of your life every month, and you will have healthy foods to eat that you don't have to think about preparing. If more than one of you is in the house, you also have alternative food options, just in case someone doesn't want to eat what you are eating.

---

[6] Erin Keller, "Americans Spend More Than 400 Hours a Year in the Kitchen: Poll," NYPost, August 3, 2022, https://nypost.com/2022/08/03/americans-spend-more-than-400-hours-a-year-in-the-kitchen-poll/

Plus, there will be no need to call out for pizza or Chinese takeout, which is unhealthy and no longer an inexpensive option for a meal.

Are you following my logic here?

Before we dive into the meat and potatoes of the strategies (food pun intended), I want to cover a few things that may be burning in your mind. One may be, "But, Wendy, I don't spend 67 minutes a day in the kitchen because I hate to cook (or think you can't cook)." If you hate it, what better reason to knock it all out once a month so you don't have to think about it anymore? If you feel you can't—sister, you've got this! My monthly meal prep recipes are so unbelievably easy that if you can walk into the kitchen and name your appliances, you can follow this plan!

That's a big part of the strategy! KEEP IT SIMPLE! You have to! It would take me an eternity to prepare a bunch of fully gourmet meals to fill my freezer, pantry, or fridge every time I meal prep! The idea is to keep this to a handful of hours so you can accomplish it much more quickly. Give yourself grace at first! It may take you 6+ hours the first time; it did me, too. Through practice, I learned that easy items are a must! Now, I LOVE to cook, so I will spend hours creating a fancy gourmet meal or an elaborate chocolate cake once in a blue moon. I reserve those things for when I'm in the mood and have time. No worries if the mood or time doesn't strike me all month because I have enough healthy meals to last! The cool thing is that those easy meals taste as I worked on them for hours, even after weeks (or months) in the freezer!

Frequently I hear people say, "I don't know HOW to change after xx years of eating like this." I will guide you step by step! If you accept the mindset shift that this new journey has to happen and are willing to follow what I teach, you will be successful. Practice makes perfect! Trust me, as you feel better and this method gets easier every month, you will never look back!

Another complaint I often hear is that it is "too cumbersome to read labels" or to learn how to eat the "natural foods" I recommend. I hear you! That can be a lot, and while it gets so much easier and becomes second nature over time, I can't stress enough that this is the key to becoming an advocate for yourself. It's my desire for you to commit to learning this skill, and there are resources that I will cover at the conclusion of this book.

Finally, folks are often concerned about being too restricted and feeling deprived. Nonsense! Clean eating is a lifestyle that encourages eating whole, natural foods, like fruits, vegetables, whole grains, healthy oils, fish, and animal proteins. Clean eating avoids processed and packaged foods containing additives, preservatives, or other chemicals. Clean eating is doable and nowhere near as restrictive as some have claimed. You will be blown away by the foods you eat and prepare, as many would not consider them "diet" foods because they aren't.

For example, I made a chocolate cake for my birthday this year that would rival any bakery! It was wholly gluten-free and void of any unnatural products or mixes. I make casseroles that would make my southern Grannie proud, and my homemade bagels and bread are always a hit! When we travel or go to events with friends, I always have extra bagel sandwiches for others, and they are constantly shocked that these delectable foods are "Wendy-approved." My Christmas treats are also always a favorite!

Would you gain weight if consuming a clean diet full of cakes, bagels, and homemade candy? 100%—YES! Even King Solomon knew many years ago that "A person without self-control is like a city with broken-down walls" (Proverbs 25:28). Watch that self-control, folks! It's this simple for this book - no one should eat cakes and cookies for every meal. But you MUST know that these foods are options and available, so you don't feel deprived. When you are eating clean, those grocery store checkout moments of "If I ate this Butterfinger before I got home, it didn't happen" aren't necessary. Not that I've ever been that girl, of course.

So, before you dive in deeper, are you ready? Are you at least open-minded and willing to learn? What I am about to teach you about living a healthy lifestyle will change your life and the lives of those you love. I say that with 100% confidence, as I've witnessed it myself with countless others. I'm teaching you to eat the foods God gave us on this earth, get away from the toxins, and then do it in a way that is possible in your busy life. And then I'm going to ask you to tell everyone too, so this truly becomes a revolution for a healthier Church!

Luke says, "Then he sent them out to tell everyone about the Kingdom of God and to heal the sick" (Luke 9:2). I may not be laying my hands on people and casting out demons. However, I have seen tremendous improvement in psychiatric disorders with proper nutrition. Instead, what I am teaching you is something the world needs to hear and can cast out diseases, aches, pains, inflammatory processes, and conditions you may / not even realize are possible to heal. The God we serve is fantastic, and the food He has provided is powerful! The strategy I teach you to follow will ensure you always have those foods around.

So, if you're in the right mindset and ready for a life change, let's do this - hand in hand. I got you!

Chapter 3

R—REALIZATION

Don't you realize that your body is the temple of the Holy Spirit, who lives in you and was given to you by God? You do not belong to yourself, for God bought you with a high price. So you must honor God with your body.

1 Corinthians 6:19-20

Likely, Christian books you have read used this passage if it was a book on health. It's so vital that it's stated twice in Scripture, nearly verbatim, as I referenced the other reference in the introduction of this book. I have used either often when I encourage good health, calling our bodies our "temples of the Holy Spirit." Paul wrote this concerning sexual sin, and while it does apply to how we treat our bodies, I look at it from a nutritional standpoint, too. For this chapter's sake, I want you to focus on the emphasis I place on the word "realize." Even two thousand years ago, he asked, "Don't you REALIZE...?" That has to be where you start in any new journey. Realization IS the mindset shift.

I am assuming that you will purge the unhealthy products from your pantry for the remainder of the book. Everyone does this differently. I'm a teetotaler, or I won't succeed, so everything had to go. Some can use a phase-out approach and phase in the new healthy items. I will leave that piece to you so I won't bore you with that minutiae. I'll simplify this by saying, "if you can't pronounce an ingredient, it likely shouldn't be consumed." There is much greater detail than that to teach, but that info will fill a whole separate book, and now I want all of the remaining focus to be on the tool to make this possible - Monthly Meal Prep.

> "And she rises while it is still night and gives food to her house-hold" (Proverbs 31:15 NASB).

This passage indicates the prep the Biblical woman went through to feed her family. But while she got up while it was still dark, the modern Proverbs 31 woman doesn't have to prepare every single day in a world where we have electricity and refrigeration. Remember that Proverbs was presented many centuries before the introduction of modern conveniences. So, plan one good meal prep day where you "get up before dawn," and the fruit of your labor will allow you to gain extra time for more than just cooking for the rest of the month!

I once read that nine out of ten people state that they have meal prepped at least once. So why don't they stick with it? I believe there may be a few reasons. First, they don't see the value in it. If you don't analyze the cost, time, and health savings, it may seem like it is not an important task to include in your life. Also, if you are simply meal prepping one time and not doing so in a way that significantly impacts what you consume over a long period, you can't realize the value. Making enough food for leftovers is considered meal prepping. So, you may have a few meals you're grateful to have planned, and then the value is gone and forgotten.

Secondly, not to be cliche, but they're probably doing it wrong! You need a systematic approach to get as much bang for your buck and your minute! What do I mean by that? I teach you to prep in such a way that will stretch every dollar you spend and maximize the most of every minute you dedicate to this life-changing exercise.

The "R" in R.I.C.H.E.S. is Realization, which is when you realize that this lifestyle is a change you absolutely can't afford NOT to make. "For we are God's masterpiece. He has created us anew in Christ Jesus, so we can do the good things he planned for us long ago" (Ephesians 2:10). As I have mentioned, God has good things He has planned for us! You are part of His beautiful masterpiece and must realize how much you physically have a role in this.

By the end of this chapter, I want you to realize how meal prep is a time saver, money saver, and health saver. Consider this as profoundly as you have time. Do a cost analysis on how much you are spending on eating out. Evaluate the nutritional value of a typical meal when you go out to eat or the pre-packaged foods you purchase. I encourage you to do whatever you need to realize that meal prepping is a game-changer in living a healthy life.

And, once you're a believer and have what I call your "awakening" when it comes to how much control you have over your health through what you choose to eat, you won't have to go through this "R" piece over and over again. It's always great to stay up to date on the latest research and studies on new chemicals added to our foods or fresh, healthy foods available on the market, but that's why I'm here! People like me who pour their whole life's work into this are here to share all we know. So, don't feel like you need to get your internet Ph.D. on healthy living unless you become extra passionate about it. Just realize that this mindset shift must happen, and I'm happy to help you take it from there.

If you are single, I'm about to teach you a game changer that will take you less time than me because you can get by on far less prep to get through a whole month. I cater all my meal prep education to the individual because I want it to be inclusive for everyone in all circumstances. If you're cooking for a family, you can scale the meals for the number you need. I also need you to listen attentively if you are part of a family but feel alone on this healthy island. You may be one of the many people reading this who says, "well, I'm ready, but my family never will be." Sis, lead by example. That's all you can do.

You also must not allow any excuse for you not to pursue this healthy path. I know it is far less convenient when you feel alone in this, but I'm going to show you that (#1) You aren't alone! There is an extensive network of us here to support you! And (#2) Meal prep is crucial for folks like you who have family who aren't as interested in pursuing this healthy journey as you are.

I have been there too. I am still there for many days! My dear husband does not follow my healthy path 100% when we travel, or he's out and about in town! However, you can bet that everything I feed him at home (most of what he eats) is clean, natural, and healthy, and I take solace in this. Plus, he loves what I cook. I often jokingly share with people when something is "Bill approved" because so many people I work with are afraid they'll make things their family won't eat. I tell them, "if my hubby loves it, that's a great barometer."

So, here's the neat thing about prepping enough food for a month. There are going to be many things that your family loves. There will also be a handful of foods you make in which they'll be less interested. They have the freedom and ability to choose what they want to eat each day. You may have occasional large casseroles you heat up for everyone or crock-pot meals made to feed four, but you might be the only one who wants it. No worries! Then it's leftovers for lunch and less for you to thaw the next couple of days! It's that simple!

I always have some of my husband's favorites on hand—Cauliflower Taco Bake, Chili, Chinese Beef and Broccoli, Meatloaf, Maple Bacon-Wrapped Pork Loin, etc. By always having these as an available option, when I want to make things I love that are less attractive to him, I don't have to feel like I can't! He just picks something else!

The last thing I'll note about having options: This means YOU ALSO have options! What a beautiful thing! When you look in your freezer and can choose from multiple options, it's like choosing from a menu of yummy items on hand all the time!

All that I've described illustrates the time savings of meal prep. Imagine how much more time you will have freed up to spend with your families in the evening if you only have to scoop food out of a crockpot or heat something in a microwave. Not to mention, the cleanup is SO much less! No more massive amounts of time doing dishes every evening. You've already dirtied the majority of the kitchenware making these meals! Now, you're just consuming them!

When meal prepping, the idea is to spend the time you would be making a meal and make many meals instead! You require little to no additional time in the preparation and will have so much more available. If this book inspires you to meal prep, healthy eating aside, and maybe you aren't ready to commit one afternoon a month to this, this principle alone will save you quite a bit of time. Every time you cook, cook lots. Save enough leftovers for 3-4 days max, and freeze the rest in individual serving containers, so you have them on hand in a pinch or for a future "no time (or desire) to cook" day. This part of the strategy alone is huge!

I have worked with many soccer moms and families with kids in many after-school activities. Many have relied for years on fast food drive-thrus to feed everyone on schedule for practice, game, or performance days. This can end, too. When you have multiple options in the freezer, the family can choose something fast to heat up, or you can have something cooking all day in the crockpot that will be a great, healthy "scoop and go" meal. Boom! No extra time is needed!

Saying this, when you don't have to feed everyone those fast food meals, you are also accomplishing the other two points of the "Realization" part of meal prepping: the money savings and the health benefits!

Sister, eating out, even at Mcdonald's, gets expensive, especially if you're doing this two, three, or five times a week during dance or ball season. According to moneygeek.com, the average fast food burger, fries, and soda in 2022 range from $6.19 at Mcdonald's to $19.95 at Five Guys.[7] So, even if you eat at Mcdonald's three times a week and get the same thing every time, a family of three spends a minimum of $55 weekly. I will teach you to make more than nine meal servings for that $55, and they will be much more nutrient dense than that fast food hamburger.

It also doesn't take a rocket scientist to tell you that fast food isn't healthy. That fast food meal - a Quarter Pounder® with Cheese, large French Fries, and large soda- costs you 1500 calories. When you eat non-nutrient-dense food, your body is not absorbing the nutrients needed to satisfy you. Items like 12-ingredient fast food fries (not just potatoes), burgers with added flavoring (to give the flavor of meat), and sodas loaded with liver-taxing high fructose corn syrup are detrimental to our health and don't have enough nutritional value to keep you from being hungry.

I teach my clients not to be calorie-focused because I can give them a 1500-calorie meal plan for an entire day. This plan, which you will never be able to finish because you will be so incredibly satisfied, is loaded with delicious high-nutrient foods. But, eating a meal from a fast food restaurant that is 1500 calories will only satisfy you for a few hours. You'll end up eating more, spending more, and gaining more health issues to satiate that hunger.

Repeated proof has been given that ingredients, such as high fructose corn syrup, cause tremendous health detriment, thus why many countries have outlawed these substances. There have been countless research studies conducted studying manufactured foods, such as the effect high fructose corn syrup and other synthetic ingredients in highly processed foods have

---

[7] Rachel Newcomb, "America's Favorite Meal Just Got A Major Price Hike," Moneygeek, September 30, 2022, https://www.moneygeek.com/living/analysis/cost-of-a-burger-by-city/

on dopamine release in the brain. People get physically addicted to processed foods in the same way they get addicted to heroin or cocaine. The addictive properties of these ingredients are another facet of our obesity and poor health epidemic. The intoxicating effects of these foods fuel the cravings and addictive behaviors that cause people to overindulge and overeat. After one week of eating natural foods, you'll be amazed that your hunger and cravings are gone or greatly diminished. Your body can use all that you are feeding it, and you will be satisfied and not overeat. It's a game-changer. If you strive to be the Proverbs 31 woman described in God's Word, remember verse 12 states, "She brings him good, not harm, all the days of her life." You can replace "him" with "them" to include your family, but I'm sure you get the idea.

I wrap up this chapter by stating a few final points. In addition to the time, money, and health savings, you will also reduce food waste, reducing the cost of what you spend on food. You are going to decrease stress from wondering what to cook, being unable to afford to eat out, or possible stress that goes along with the thought that you simply don't want to cook. If you already have items prepared ahead, all that stress just disappears. And because you're eating healthy, nutrient-dense foods, you will be full and satisfied and may even reduce the portion sizes you eat, saving even more! Win, win, win!

Before we move on, sister, consider this: Still referencing the actions of the Proverbs woman, "Strength and dignity are her clothing, and she smiles at the future" (Proverbs 31:25 NASB). Be strong. Be dignified. God is with you so you can "smile at your future," and since He has provided the excellent sustenance we need, being unhealthy doesn't need to rob you of your strength and dignity to complete His mission for your life.

If I need to enlist the help of folks I've worked with to convince you that now is the time to start this healthy life, don't skip the following section with my client testimonials! Otherwise, let's get ready for your action items to begin in the next chapter!

CLIENT HEALTHY EATING AND "LIFESTYLE TRANSFORMATION" TESTIMONIALS

I have been fighting my weight for as long as I can remember. The past six months with you have been an eye-opening experience and journey for both Gina and me. Your "program" is not a diet; it is an education in nutrition and how it affects the body as a whole. Rather than focusing on weight loss, you have helped me to remain focused on wellness. This is a life-changing journey we are on with you, and we are so blessed to have found you, and the help you have provided and continue to provide is transformative.

—J. Tony R., Boerne, TX

I joined Wendy's 16-week healthy eating program, and my life has forever changed for the positive. I encouraged my wife to join me on the journey, and within 16 weeks, we both lost 20 pounds each. However, it was the mindset and lifestyle change that was the most transformational. We can never think of food (especially processed) the same way again. We constantly look for the most healthy alternatives. Wendy's advice on how to read labels and eat healthy while continuing to live our lives helped us far more than the other weight and nutrition programs we've tried. Wendy gets it! She really knows how people are motivated, and she tailored her approach to our specific situation. The program was a God-send that helped us feel better and live better.

—Ted K., Herndon, VA

Thanks to Wendy's clean eating program and mentoring, I was able to lose 30 pounds and have kept it off for two years by continuing to follow the clean eating lifestyle. I no longer have chronic pain or fatigue, a battle for over a decade, and have completely eliminated all pain medications! Once we figured out my trigger foods, my hot flashes disappeared, and my perimenopause (which came on way too early) was reversed! Wendy's guidance is the real deal. I'm so thankful I have my life back!

—A.P., Powhatan, VA

Through Wendy's program, my A1C of 6.4 dropped to 5.4, keeping me away from diabetes. I have come off my blood pressure medication, and my cholesterol has improved. I lost 30 lbs along the way and am still working on losing more. I made my health issues a priority, and losing weight along the way was a bonus. Wendy made that easy. We did not discuss my weight and celebrated together as my clothes size started getting smaller. The biggest gain is learning what to look for in the ingredients that are in our foods. I enjoy finding new items in the grocery store and trying new recipes. I love the way I feel now that I have been eating clean. I enjoy the newfound energy that I have and being able to sleep at night. Thank you, Wendy, for giving me my life back.

—Shelley B., Moseley, VA

When I joined you on your Clean Eating program in August 2021, I was a mess! I had retired two months prior, and I was a 69-year-old obese, fatigued, sleep-deprived woman with chronic debilitating foot pain and a chronic cough. Both the foot pain and cough had lasted for many years, with no relief despite trips to physicians. I had been diagnosed with asthma and prescribed inhalers, which only slightly helped, but never eliminated my cough. In less than a week of being on the elimination phase of your program, my foot pain was gone, as was my cough about a week later. We quickly learned that dairy is a huge inflammatory trigger for me, as my foot pain returned almost immediately after the reintroduction of cheese and then vanished after once again eliminating it. I live my life dairy free now and have had many friends and even strangers with whom I've shared my story say they would die and could never give up cheese. To those folks, I always say that to be free of foot pain and chronic cough, it is little to give up. I miss absolutely nothing in eating clean and eliminating dairy, as I have learned quick, easy and delicious substitutes. I've also lost weight and cannot remember when I felt this great. Wendy, I know I would not be this healthy if I had not joined this program. You provide us with all we need to know to live a healthy life.

—Joy H., S Chesterfield, VA

I started working with Wendy just three weeks ago, and I am AMAZED by the results so far. My sleep and mood have improved, and I have a lot more energy throughout the day (no more 3 pm crash!). These changes have already made a huge difference in my life. I am just getting started in this journey, so I know the physical changes will come, but as of right now, I'm down 8 pounds from my starting weight, which brings me 8 pounds closer to my goal weight. The non-physical changes have meant the most to me, though; it's awesome to see your life improve before your eyes through simple swaps and changes.

—Brittany G., Taneytown, MD

At the start of the New Year in 2022, I found myself face to face with the fact that if I didn't do something about my ongoing weight problem soon, I would still be here in January 2023, wondering why I was still fat. I met Wendy on my friend's Facebook post about how this program had helped her not only lose weight but lose some chronic health problems as well. It took me 61 years of trying every diet, every fad, the grapefruit diet, shakes, keto, Weight Watchers, etc., only to never be successful. I could never sustain it and went back to eating junk and negated any loss I had made. Wendy taught me how to eat the right way, the clean way, eating foods I already loved. I started the 16-week Lifestyle Transformation Program, followed the meal plans, passed all my trigger food tests, and by the end of the 16 weeks, I had lost 30 lbs. I took the tools I had learned in the program and continued on my own, and to date, I have lost an additional 18 lbs, for a total of 48 lbs. The program has given me a new relationship with food; I no longer feel like if I pass on something, I'm missing out. I can always have it another day if it doesn't fit into my macros for the day. I can honestly say I know I will never gain the weight back or go back to the way I used to eat...I just don't want to put certain foods in my body anymore. For instance, I now drink my organic coffee black, with only a small amount of monk fruit sweetener. And I was the Coffee-mate queen! Now, when I drink my coffee, I actually taste and enjoy the coffee instead of the fake creamer! I've decreased my blood pressure meds, dropped three sizes in clothing, and lost inches everywhere. I never feel like I'm missing out! Wendy has taught me all these things, and I am so grateful for the education and information I have gained from her...She came into my life at a time when God knew I needed her...and somehow, I can't help but think that my precious Momma may have had a heavenly hand in it as well!

—Mary Beth B., Colonial Heights, VA

I started working with Massey Wellness after I reached my highest weight of 250 pounds. I had tried losing weight several times, and I was not even able to work out around three times per week. My main problem was eating poorly. After signing up with Wendy in January 2021, things changed. Wendy's dedication to helping me was amazing. From weekly menus detailing everything that I needed to purchase and how to prepare my meals was so easy. I'd like to add that even if I had questions about anything, she was just a message, email, or phone call away. Her attention to detail helped ease my mind when I had questions. I'm just finishing up my 23rd month with her. So far, I'm down 50 pounds, off my blood pressure and cholesterol medications, and am no longer pre-diabetic. My blood work was normal after just a couple of months with her. I have a ton of energy and average walking 9 miles a day. Something I couldn't do before

I signed up. Thank you, Wendy, for helping me get my life under control. I appreciate it more than you may ever understand.

—Aaron S., Odenton, MD

Wendy's 16-week program really opened my eyes to the importance of reading labels and understanding them. I had no idea there were so many harmful ingredients in foods that appear to be "healthy" and "good for you." While I'm not perfect in my pursuit of clean eating, I am much more knowledgeable and selective in what I choose to put in my mouth. Once you start eating "real" food, you learn to appreciate how good it truly tastes and realize how most "bad" processed and genetically modified food actually tastes like chemicals.

—Amy F., Glen Allen, VA

Chapter 4

I—INVENTORY/IDENTIFY

*She carefully watches everything in her household
and suffers nothing from laziness.*

Proverbs 31:27

Ok, you're in the mindset, and you realize it's time to jump into this new world of meal prepping. Now, what do you cook?

I CAN NOT STAND being wasteful, so the first thing I'm going to tell you is to take an inventory of what you currently have:

- Do you have any freezer meals left from last month that you won't eat by the time you prep for the next month?
- Do you have any frozen meats you recently picked up in a sale that need a plan?
- Do you have any frozen fruits or veggies that need to be used to clear space for freezer meals?
- Do you have any grains on hand that you wouldn't need to purchase - rice, quinoa, chickpea pasta, etc.?
- Do you have any sauces or canned goods that need a plan for use?

- Which healthy flour and sugars do you already have on hand?
- How about baking and snack possibilities? Dates? Nuts? Cacao nibs? Coconut flakes? Enjoy Life chocolate chips? (The best, trust me!) Chia seeds? Flax meal?
- How many fresh veggies and fruits do you have on hand that need immediate attention? Do any of them need to be frozen until your meal prep day, or will you use them between now and then?

It makes so much more sense to shop in your pantry and freezer for what you already have first. This practice is your most significant money savings right out of the gate! I used to be someone who massively shopped the sales, and then items would go to waste because I'd forget I bought ten cans of organic chickpeas. Make it a practice to do this every month. Shopping the sales in a big way is a fantastic idea, particularly when you're blessed to find great deals on healthy pantry items because that can be a rarity. However, this only works if you use what you purchase!

Plus, when you do this, you'll clear space in your freezer for these excellent meals you'll prepare ahead!

Next, how many meals do you need to prepare?

- Are you the only one eating?
- If your family eats with you, will they eat all meals or just supper?
- How many meals a day do you eat? With my clients' intermittent fasting, many only eat two meals daily with a snack. But, if you're a grazer or a three-meal, two-snack-a-day person, the number of meals on hand needs to reflect this.
- Are you going to eat the previous night's leftovers for lunch the next day or for supper a couple of days in a row? If so, consider how many servings you need for supper, including lunches.
- Are you going to be home for the whole month, or are you traveling at all?

- If you are traveling, will you have a kitchen, and can you take a cooler if driving?

- Do you have any planned times when you don't need to have a meal at home? Brunch on Tuesday mornings with your Ladies' Bible Study? Date night with hubby? Lunch after church at Aunt Judy's house every Sunday? These are all meals for which you don't have to plan.

- If this is new to you, and you're restricting yourself from excessive eating out, are you planning to be a teetotaler? Or are you giving yourself one or two meals to go out per month? There is no wrong answer, but you'll want to plan accordingly.

Now that you know how many meals you need to plan for, you'll want to note breakfast, lunch, and supper separately. Of course, unless you need no division and can eat pork chops for breakfast and drink smoothies for supper. Some people are good with that! No judgment!

It's now time to plan what you're going to fix. Start with what you have and what's easy:

- If you have frozen fruit, how many smoothies can you make with what you have?

- If you have frozen veggies and meat, what will go together? For example, if you have beef stew cubes and a bag of frozen broccoli, that's the makings of the start of a good stew.

- If you have plenty of almond flour, what is your favorite easy recipe you make with that? What additional ingredients for that recipe do you have on hand, and what do you need? Still want to make it, or do you want to find a new almond flour recipe?

- Do you have chickpea pasta on hand? How about canned tomatoes? That sounds like a great reason to meal-prep homemade pasta sauce!

Next, check your sales circulars or your local grocery store's website for their sale items. If you see something you know you can use, that jumps out at you and is an excellent price, go for that!

Do you use Misfits Market, Thrive Market, or other online discount food stores? I find some of my absolute best deals on pantry items on Thrive and the best meat and produce values on Misfits, so I always check both. Compare these to your grocery store because you may find better options locally.

If you are a member of a farm co-op or have gotten to know any of your local farms, they will often have specials like "Frugal Friday" as they're trying to move products to make room for new items coming in season. Co-ops often have special sales for their members, so be sure to get to know those specials because that can give you some other ideas for your upcoming meal prep menu.

When you've exhausted all of these money-saving ideas to determine what you're going to prepare, it's time to go back to your list and see how many more meals you need to plan.

KEEP IT SIMPLE! Your goal for your meal prep day is to make as many meals in as little time as possible. You will make your life much easier if you don't mind many repeats and leftovers. But be honest with yourself. If you can't tolerate repeating something more than once in two weeks, you'll need to plan way more options to have prepped ahead than someone like me, who could eat the same thing every day and not get bored.

Before you think you're taking advice from someone who eats to that level of boredom, no, ma'am! I said I *could* eat the same thing every day. I most definitely do not, and that's so that I don't lose my family's interest in my meals. I always have a lot of options and variety.

Consider the following when choosing how to fill your remaining open meal plan slots. First, you can skip committing to when you intend to cook each meal. Once meals are prepped and frozen, one of the beautiful things about this lifestyle is the freedom it gives you to "wing it!" All we're doing at this stage is determining HOW MUCH is necessary.

Plan to prepare breakfast items, such as egg bites, chia puddings, a breakfast casserole, and sausage balls. All can be refrigerated for around four days or frozen and then thawed and reheated well. Another huge time saver is to have smoothie ingredients all cut and frozen ahead in individual bags, so you just need to dump them in a blender when ready. These and the chia puddings can make great breakfasts or snacks.

What time of year is it, and what kind of cooking might you prefer? If it's summertime and you love to grill out on the weekends, plan to prep some marinated chicken or steaks for some of your meals, and just have some steam-in-bags of veggies on hand for those nights. Maybe plan to pull out the rice cooker and cook some brown rice while you're on the grill. Easy options, as suggested, are still relatively hands-off. You won't believe the flavor you'll get from a freezer bag of raw chicken thighs, freshly squeezed lemon, and minced garlic when it's thawed and grilled! Oh, the joy! You just wait!

Plan at least one big pot or casserole of something: chili, a nice hearty soup, a big batch of pasta sauce, a pot of beans and greens (yes, my southern is showing), chili-mac, cauliflower taco bake, etc. One of these hearty meals is a significant part of the strategy to fix something the whole family will love when there may be other items they won't. It is also suitable for those days when you run out the door in a hurry and forget or don't have time to throw something in the slow cooker.

I always make a no-bean chili, or pasta sauce, because if I decide to make Hawaiian Chicken in the slower cooker, which my husband dislikes, I have zero guilt as I still get to enjoy one of my favorite meals. He has chili or plenty of other options available. With this pot or casserole of whatever you choose, plan to freeze a bunch of individual or double servings so that they are quick to reheat in the microwave without having to reheat a massive amount of something. Remember, you can always reheat a few if you need more, but reheating too much of something is a commitment you don't want to make in a rush. As soon as you heat a large item, you're stuck for days with the same food if you don't want to waste it.

Plan some desserts that will freeze well in individual servings. These don't have to be a planned daily consumption. Cheesecake bites, cookies, fat bombs, homemade candy bars, etc., are all great options, but know your limits! I make limited amounts of these because I plan to put them in the back of the freezer (out of sight, out of mind). When I have a craving, with a bit of digging, I can pull out a single cookie and let it thaw out. Those extra steps keep me in check, so I don't overdo it. If those cookies are on the counter, they will be too tempting, and I'm not letting the enemy in like that!

A typical monthly meal prep day (4 hours), for me, accomplishes all of these:

- Ten breakfasts of a variety of smoothies
- Ten breakfasts of a hot breakfast (egg bites, breakfast casserole, sausage balls)
- 20 breakfasts/snacks of a variety of chia puddings
- One dozen sliced bagels or other homemade bread on hand for sandwiches
- Eight freezer meals for the slow cooker (with leftovers)
- 4-8 marinated meats to be baked, grilled, air-fried, pan-fried, or slow-cooked.
- The exact amount of frozen steam-in-bag veggies (4-8) unless it's summer and I have many fresh ones from my garden.
- One large casserole or pot of something that makes at least 16 individual servings.

Great job! Now you've decided on the "what!" Keep reading, and we'll tackle "when" you're going to do all this fantastic meal prep!

Chapter 5

C—CALENDAR

But the Holy Spirit produces this kind of fruit in our lives: love, joy,
peace, patience, kindness, goodness, faithfulness, gentleness, and
self-control. There is no law against these things!

Galatians 5:22-23

Sister, though I could give you evidence of all nine, the two qualities of the Fruit of the Spirit that this entire book should have you focusing on are faithfulness and self-control, especially when it comes to determining when to schedule your meal prep time. Faithfulness to planning and self-control to avoid procrastination is imperative. You can do this! And once you get through your first month and receive back the large number of hours gained in exchange for your handful of hours sacrificed, you will be a believer, and this step will become much easier the next time.

I was whining once about not having enough hours in the day to a business mentor. She told me, "24 hours is the great equalizer. We all have the same amount of time for what we prioritize." Wow. And just when I was about to give her the "you don't understand, I'm different" speech, she said, "And no one is different. We all have the same 24 hours." Ouch. Ok. It wasn't the lack of hours in the day. I could not prioritize properly. And that had to change. When I made that statement, I averaged 5 hours of sleep and was constantly spinning my wheels. Since my transformation, I now sleep 7-8 hours a night and have plenty of time to accomplish all I need. So what changed? I learned to live smart, not hard, and meal prep fits perfectly with this.

As I shared earlier, by incorporating my simple meal prep strategies into your routine, you will get back 24 hours a month of your life! The first month is the hardest, but you can do this. Start by planning a 6-hour block—yes, all in one day is a must—and know that you will get faster and be able to reduce this in time.

Do you want to do this on the weekend? A weekday when the kids are at school? Early morning? Late in the evening? Do you wish to schedule this with a friend so you can keep each other motivated? There are no wrong answers to any of these questions; you just need to determine the best plan for you and stick to it.

Do you still believe you don't have time? Here's a painful but necessary exercise I did when I had "no time" yet needed to make changes. I started paying attention to what was sucking my time away from me—scrolling on social media, binge-watching Netflix, playing Candy Crush, and surfing Amazon. If you have an iPhone, it has an average daily screen time counter. My number was staggering!

Since most of my business is virtual and I rely heavily on social media, I had to recognize that just because I was on social media didn't mean I was being productive. Often I went on social media for a specific work-related reason, and like a squirrel chasing shiny objects, two hours were gone the next time I knew it. I ended up purchasing a phone with only calling and texting; my immediate family members are the only ones with my number. I set myself "office hours" for my "work phone" and social media, so that distraction disappeared. What a tremendous gift I was able to give back to myself! Of course, not everyone needs a second phone to accomplish this, as our situations may differ.

My point is: Do what you have to do! Ask God for help in this area if you need to.

> In view of all this, make every effort to respond to God's promises. Supplement your faith with a generous provision of moral excellence, and moral excellence with knowledge, and knowledge with self-control, and self-control with patient endurance.
>
> —2 Peter 1:5-6

Ask The Holy Spirit to guide your steps so you can free up the space you need for this new healthy lifestyle.

Changes like this will be earth-shattering to you if you constantly believe there is never enough time. Start with awareness and work to create space for what truly matters and what you will prioritize in your life. If you picked up this book, then feeding your family healthily in a way that saves time is at least a desired priority, and that's a significant first step.

Your meal prep period must be an uninterrupted block of time, hence my stress earlier that it all be in one day. Why does it matter? Because your kitchen is going to look like a bomb went off! I'm here to tell you that if I had to clean that up and then do it again the next day - it's never going to happen. Period. Knock it all out in one day; feel massively accomplished, and then don't stress over it again!

One other thing to consider as you plan is your budget, as that may be a factor concerning which day you choose. Remember to save aside some of your typical weekly grocery budgets for your big meal prep grocery trip. This practice can free up the money for some of the new ingredients you will purchase, as you will lessen eating out. As I mentioned in the previous chapter, start by shopping your pantry when determining what you will make each month. Rather than constantly purchasing new items, this will help immensely. If you are completely overhauling your home to a healthy eating lifestyle, you may have a lot of things to replace in your pantry. The first month or two may seem steep, but this will significantly improve. If you're not ready to jump feet first into the clean, healthy eating lifestyle, meal prep is a great start! Use the inventory that you already have on hand! When it's time to restock, choose an alternate, healthier option.

Alright, so you have the date scheduled, written on your calendar, and a friend joining you if you choose. Let's move on to the Harvest.

Chapter 6

H—HARVEST

*Yes, the Lord pours down his blessings. Our land
will yield its bountiful harvest.*

Psalm 85:12

Now that you know what and when you are going to meal prep, it's time to gather your supplies!

The first part of this chapter will serve the person who has never done this before, and it may seem overwhelming. I am going to give you a list of non-food supplies. Focus on the "must-haves." Worry about the "nice to haves" and "next level" items as you're ready and able to step into those. I didn't have some of those items for the first ten years of meal prepping. Do not look at this list and run. You can do this!

Recommended equipment

1. **Large waterproof adhesive labels OR a good Sharpie pen! (Must Have)**

   I prefer just writing in Sharpie on the plastic bags, but you go with what makes you happy for your organization level.

2. **3x5 notecards or similar size post-it notes. (Must Have)**

I use these to organize the ingredients I will use for each recipe, especially for freezer meals.

3. **Canning Funnel. (Must Have)**

This item is vital for making homemade broths, stocks, and soups and storing them in your canning jars. It makes the job much more manageable than pouring directly into the jars.

4. **A slow cooker. (Must Have)**

If you only choose one item I recommend adding to your kitchen, get a large capacity slow cooker.

You can get one relatively inexpensively. Prices start around $49 (8 quarts) and go up from there in capacity and cost. I recommend you buy the largest you can afford. Save your money on something other than a two or three-quart one, even if you are single. They are close in price, and you will need more room than what they offer for many of the meals you will be prepping.

There are also plenty of pressure cookers that double as slow cookers. If you want a pressure cooker and have a larger budget, get a combo for the extra features, but this is unnecessary to begin your journey!

5. **Canning jars and Freezer Safe Glass Containers - a variety of sizes. (Must Have)**

You can't have too many of these. These will be SO IMPORTANT, so you can have plenty of prepared food ready to reheat or thaw. Make it a point to have lots of containers to freeze single-serving meals without having to thaw a whole bulk meal at a time. On the nights everyone in your home is running in different directions, everyone can choose meals to their liking and grab whatever they desire out of the freezer if you have them in single servings.

6. **All sizes of freezer-safe zipper bags. (Must Have)**

These bags are a must unless you only plan to vacuum-seal every-thing, and then you'll need to add lots of bags to your supply of vacuum sealer accessories.

I use gallon-size bags only for my freezer meals. I also utilize quart, sandwich-sized, and snack bags to portion out trail mixes, cut veggies, fruit, egg bites, desserts, etc.

If you are interested in using less plastic in your home, consider reusable freezer bags.

7. **Hands-Free Baggy Racks. (Must Have)**

GAME CHANGER! I only recently discovered these little plastic lifesavers! You can hold open multiple bags at once while filling them without creating an extra mess! What a time AND mess saver, especially when making your freezer meals!

8. **An extra freezer. (Nice to Have)**

If you are new to meal prepping, you may have your standard fridge/freezer combo in your kitchen. If you have any space in a basement, mud room, garage, or anywhere, get a separate freezer! I love my large chest freezer, which was brand new when we bought it; however, before this fantastic addition to our home, I had free ones or super cheap ones that I would pick up used. Check flea markets, Craigslist, Facebook Marketplace pages, etc. Someone is always trying to upgrade theirs, downsize, or eliminate one from their home that works just fine! I spent years never spending over $50 on one—I even scored a couple for free!

You may also consider a smaller freezer as a "nice to have" item and then upgrade to a huge one as a "next level" plan to position you to be able to purchase half cows from a local farm, etc., to reduce your meat budget drastically.

9. **A vacuum sealer. (Next Level)**

I have operated for so many years without one, but what a GREAT way to extend the freshness and life of items you meal prep, whether you're making items for the fridge, freezer, or pantry.

If you don't have or decide not to spend money on one of these, you can use zipper bags and glass containers.

10. **A breadmaker. (Next Level)**

Again, not required, but this is an excellent tool for making homemade gluten-free bread, so you can still enjoy sandwiches, sliced bread with meals, etc., and always know what is in your creations.

Make sure you get one with a gluten-free setting, as the rising process for gluten-free bread is different (not more challenging, just different) than regular yeast bread.

11. **A canner. (Next Level)**

A canner is not a requirement but a purchase for the next-level meal prepper.

You can purchase a water bath canner for a much lower cost than a large pressure canner, which is appropriate for most items you want to can and store. Consider a large-capacity pressure canner if you are interested in canning meat, soups with meat, stocks, or more acidic vegetables.

Also, purchase some good basic "how-to" canning books if you are new to canning. I learned a lot of what I know from older family members, but printed references always give you a new perspective on some tips you may not know, and there are lots of tips and tricks to canning. It is a worthwhile cost-saving endeavor that will also make you feel good that you know where the ingredients are coming from in your canned foods.

Ok, now that you've harvested your kitchen supplies, we need to harvest the food! Before I share the minutiae of the details by which I bargain shop, if you're one to get a headache over such information, please do some calming breathing exercises and then keep reading. The purpose of this book is to teach you how to do what I do, so just hang in there with me, and I'll get you through it. If you are not someone who cares to be or plans to be budget conscious, then my bargain-shopping suggestions are something you can just skim right over.

Make a list of every item you need on your monthly meal prep day. Separate the non-perishable from the perishable items on your list and know where your best options for purchase typically are.

Once you construct your list, even if you're a couple of weeks out from your planned meal prep day, you can start looking for non-perishable items. Unless cost isn't a concern for you, this is when I recommend comparison shopping. Now, do not let this overwhelm you. Pick one or two online resources you prefer—I like Thrive Market and Amazon best for shelf-stable items. And I start going down my list on both apps to see which one has what I need at the best price, and I write it down on my list. So, "Aroy-D Coconut Milk—Amazon $22.61 six 16.9 oz cartons." This way, when I take my list to my grocery store, I will determine the best place to purchase it.

I refuse to overwhelm myself with too many options in town, so if it's not available and less expensive in either my favorite closest grocery store or big box store, I'm not driving all over town. I don't have time for it, and that's not how I want to spend my extra 24 hours a month. Luckily, this doesn't change much from month to month unless there is an excellent sale in your local store. Usually, if you find it relatively cheaper online, it will always be. Once you get used to what those items are, this process becomes much quicker.

Make sure you're giving yourself adequate time for this step, as you may need to wait several days for your items to arrive in the mail. Early shopping also helps me budget better because I can buy the "dry" goods a week or two before my big meat and produce purchases.

When making your lists, consider your budget and which conveniences, if any, you are willing and able to spend extra. You may not be able to choose convenience, but shortcuts are available for some items if you are. I am super thrifty, so I don't mind cutting up my meat sometimes when I need strips or cubes, but it would be a time saver if you purchase already cubed or stripped beef. One item I am willing to pay for convenience is fruit for my smoothies and chia puddings. I buy big bags of already cut frozen organic fruit in my local big box store, and it is a MASSIVE time saver over what I would spend cutting fruit during meal prep. Also, many stores have already cut fresh veggies in their produce section, but they are usually quite a bit more pricey, so just decide if that's a price you're willing to spend. There is no wrong answer to this. Just know your budget and what value you place on the time it will save to purchase these items.

For perishable items, I always have three different possibilities. First, I'm blessed to live in a rural area with a few fantastic farms I love and trust. Summer farmers' markets are a wonderful time and place to get the opportunity to meet some of these fine, hardworking farmers if you don't already know them. If they have on-site farm stores convenient for you, visit them! I do this for a few different reasons, primarily because it gets you closer to where your food is raised.

Many of these farms have co-ops, which are membership opportunities where you are providing them money up front to belong to a "club." They offer savings and great discounts, special members-only sales, etc., throughout their harvest season. Farms vary in expense, but when the budget allows, I prefer to see where my meat comes from, and the quality is generally far superior to the grocery stores. Plus, supporting your local farmer is always a great idea when you can!

Second, I check the prices on Misfits Market online. Again, this is the online resource I prefer, but I know plenty of folks who shop other online meat sources, "Butcher Box," "Seven Sons Farms," etc. Make the decision that works best for you, and stick to one. I love Misfits because I can get reasonable prices on organic meat, eggs, cheese, nitrite-free bacon, no preservative sausage, and a fantastic produce selection. Also, with Misfits, you can schedule your delivery day to a day that works for you. I recommend the day before you plan to meal prep. Also, I love that I have a 3-day shopping window, so I can put all of the cold items I need in my virtual shopping cart on Misfits and jot down the prices I'm paying. Then I head to my third option.

Remember earlier when I suggested you research the discounting schedule for your local butcher or meat department? Head to your store (as close to your meal prep day as possible, but before you have to purchase your Misfits order) and see if any of your meat, dairy, or produce items you need are less expensive in your store. If they are, get them, but ensure you have room in your freezer if you are more than a few days from your meal prep day.

Here is how I purchase my cold food:

My Misfits shopping window is Sunday through Tuesday every week. Sunday or Monday, I will put everything in my virtual cart and make a note of the prices. Tuesday morning, my grocery store butcher marks everything down. I go to the grocery store early that Tuesday morning and purchase drastically reduced items from my list if it's less than Misfits. Once I get home and put everything in the fridge, I'll return to the online shopping cart, delete the items I no longer need from Misfits, and complete my order.

My order will arrive on Friday, and my meal prep day is Saturday. If I need to change my meal prep day, I adjust all of this, but this schedule works best to ensure I have as much of my meat fresh when it is time to prep.

According to the USDA, refrigerate raw ground meats, poultry, seafood, and variety meats (liver, tongue, chitterlings, etc.) only 1 to 2 days before either cooking or freezing. Beef, veal, lamb, and pork roasts, steaks, and chops may be kept for 3 to 5 days.[8]

If the specials on the ground beef and chicken were just too good to pass up in my grocery store, I will go ahead and throw them in the freezer when I get home, and I will minimally thaw them, just enough to work with them when I need them on meal prep day if I intend to prep raw and refreeze. You don't want to keep thawing and refreezing meat, as it will affect the taste, but thawing chicken just enough to break apart pieces from each other, if necessary, and then quickly refreezing when you have prepped will not harm them.

Are you excited to compare shops and get rolling on this step, or have I given you the headache of which I warned you? Luckily for you, I love this stuff! I'm a former "crazy couponer," and finding deals gets me super crazy excited. I know I'm unique and not necessarily the average shopper out there. I just want you to know there are options to keep it more thrifty, and my routine works for me. You have to find your groove.

> They sow their fields, plant their vineyards, and harvest their bumper crops. How he blesses them! They raise large families there, and their herds of livestock increase.
>
> —Psalm 107:37-38

---

[8] US Department of Agriculture, "How Long Can I Keep Meat in the Refrigerator: Knowledge Article," USDA, July 17, 2019, https://ask.usda.gov/s/article/How-long-can-I-keep-meat-in-the-refrigerator#~:text=For%20raw%20ground%20meats%2C%20poultry,kept%203%20to%205%20days.:

Chapter 7

E—EXECUTE

*Remember, it is sin to know what you ought to do
and then not do it.*

James 4:17

A m I saying it's a sin not to meal prep? Absolutely not! That would be crazy! All I'm stating is if you have learned an easier way to provide healthy, nutrient-dense meals for your family and harvested all of the supplies and ingredients to make it happen, all you need to do is carry out that plan. My goodness, don't stop now!

It's the day before your big day! The big day you've been planning, likely for weeks, to get here! Here are all the steps I take the day before, often while I'm just on the couch watching a movie with my hubby. (You can do this part anytime before your meal prep day, but I always enjoy this exercise the day before because it gets me in the mindset of what the next day will entail.)

Gather some 3x5 note cards or similar-size post-it notes, your gallon-size freezer bags, and a Sharpie pen or waterproof labels you plan to make. Also, have the list you've constructed with your plan handy. Go ahead and jot down the title of what you're creating on each note card and how many items you plan to make. "24 egg bites," "4 Chinese Beef & Broccoli," etc.

Start with your freezer meals. I like to list the ingredients I will place in each freezer meal bag on the notecard for each one. After you fill out one, grab the number of zipper bags you need or labels, and fill out the instructions for that dish.

Many simply read, "Hawaiian Chicken (date prepared), Slow cook for 6-8 hours." That will be it. Some will be a little more extensive, like "Chinese Beef and Broccoli (date prepared), Slow cook for 8 hours. In the last 30 minutes, stir in 3 cups of fresh broccoli. Serve over rice."

You must be able to grab this item from the freezer weeks from now, know what it is, the date you prepared it, and the basic instructions to make it that day. Often when I'm skimming my freezer at night before I go to bed to decide which freezer meal to place in the fridge to begin to thaw overnight, I consider my craziness or lack thereof the next day. Am I only going to have the bandwidth to dump something in a slow cooker and turn it on? Will I have the time and energy to add broccoli and throw rice in the rice cooker before eating? If I know the next day is jam-packed with appointments, I will grab something with the fewest instructions, and then I will only have to spend 30 seconds in the morning on my family's meal.

For items that aren't freezer meals, you don't have to re-write your recipes on your 3x5 cards if you have them in a particular place you store them. On one of these cards, I may just write:

6 Blueberry Chia Pudding

5¼ cups almond milk

1 cup chia seeds

⅓ cup maple syrup

3 cups blueberries

¾ cups slivered almonds

See phone

⑥ Blueberry Chia Pudding

5 1/4 cup almond milk
1 cup chia seeds
1/3 cup maple syrup
3 cups blueberries
3/4 cup slivered almonds

*see phone

I keep many recipes on my phone "notes" app, so I will not rewrite them. This method works for me. You may choose to rewrite or to note which cookbook you have this recipe in. I will simply write the ingredients so I know what to gather, and then go ahead and alert myself to where the recipe is.

The final step I do the night before is to note the "like" ingredients. Adding this to my pre-work is a reasonably new step I started last year, and it's made an enormous difference in the organization of my products, especially my freezer meals. I'll thumb through my completed 3x5 cards and put a number in parenthesis for however many different recipes I'm using that item in. For example, if I'm using coconut aminos in three varied recipes, I'm going to put next to coconut aminos on that card a "(3)." This way, when I've put coconut aminos in all three recipes the next day, I will put it away. This practice has helped my clutter and clean up drastically since I began doing this.

Doing all this prep work the day before, a week earlier, or even in the morning of your big day will keep you focused and organized while preparing your meals. You can certainly choose to skip this pre-work, but if I miss it, I can guarantee it will take an extra 1-2 hours for my ADHD brain to organize each recipe as I go. Worth it to knock this out!

Okay! It's showtime! Think back to the beginning of this book when I asked you to consider the ants! "Ants—they aren't strong, but they store up food all summer" (Proverbs 30:25). If you aren't feeling it today, dear sister, let's shake that off and do this anyway! Today you're the ant and the Proverbs 31 woman all wrapped up into one. "She dresses for work, rolls up her sleeves, eager to get started" (Proverbs 31:17 MSG). You've got this!

It should go without saying, but you must start with a clean slate. If you have dishes in the sink, clutter on the counters, or if you still need to sort this past week's mail which has been piling up, get rid of it all. Clean the dishes, start the dishwasher, and clear your countertops of everything you won't need.

My kitchen doesn't have much storage, so my small appliances live on my counter. On meal prep day, I temporarily relocate all of the machines I will not use for my meal prep day to my office. Do whatever you need to clear your space for the next several hours. You will thank me later. If you keep unnecessary things around when you are elbow-deep into this exercise, the clutter will give you anxiety—at least, it does me. This mental health step is a must-do.

Give yourself a staging area - an area where you are going to do most of your prep. It could be an island, a particular section of your counter, or whatever place you will be most comfortable with and have a decent amount of space. This area needs to stay spotless while you work all day, and this will be the primary area you will continuously work and then clean. The rest of the kitchen will get your attention later.

Next, gather all the supplies you need, leaving the frozen fruits, meats, etc., in the fridge and freezer. Pull out all your dry goods, fruits, and veggies that are fine to be out of the fridge—for example, potatoes, onions, and apples. Keep those nearby but in a separate area from your staging area. You can quickly grab them, but they won't be in your way while you're prepping.

If you plan to make a large batch of stock during this time, go ahead and load up your slow cooker(s) with your stock ingredients, as that will cook well beyond your meal prep day (12-72 hours, per your preference). I like to start a batch on this day because I don't want to have my slow cookers in use for days at a time during the month when I may need to use one for one of my freezer meals. Completing this now removes a potential complication later. If you plan to use your bones and veggie scraps from today's prep for the stock, then this can undoubtedly be the last thing you do. Either way, it's great to knock out during a few days when you'll have freshly cooked food on hand, and there's no need for the slow cooker.

Next, begin creating whatever your large pot or casserole dish will be. If I'm making chili or soup, I want it to cook for some time for the flavors to meld together before I freeze it. If it's ready before I can store it, I turn it down at a low temperature, and it won't hurt anything. Plus, if the family gets hungry while I'm still meal prepping, "soup's on!"

Next, make the easy dry items to get them out of the way. Trail mixes, individually measured baggies of nuts, dry mix-ins for raspberry-walnut snacks, bulk taco seasoning, bulk pancake mix, and the like. Once you make all of these items, you will usually have quite a few ingredients that can go back into the cupboard, and you will know this if you note that on your 3x5 card ahead of time.

Your casserole is done or soon-to-be by this time. Now it's time to start your baked items; bagels, egg bites, breakfast casserole, sausage balls, cookies, etc. If you have multiple of these items to make (I usually try to limit myself to two to four, and recommend when you are new to this, starting with two), then make as many of these items as you can and have them ready to go in the oven, consecutively. So when you complete one, replace it with the next. Some things freeze well-baked or unbaked. For example, if you choose to freeze a breakfast casserole or sausage balls that you've prepped but not baked, write the instructions for the day you plan to bake them on the container. Hopefully, you completed this in your pre-work.

While your items are baking, knock out the next most easy-to-accomplish thing on your list, your smoothies! These are so easy and such a time saver to have prepped ahead! When all you have to do in the morning is dump two bags of fruits and veggies into a blender with coconut water and hit "start," you'll be glad there are no more early morning produce-cutting sessions for your healthy lifestyle. I like the consistency of my smoothies when half the fruit is frozen and half thawed, so if I'm making ten smoothies ahead, I'm assembling 20 bags of frozen fruit and veggies. This way, I can thaw one of the baggies in the fridge the night before or on the counter when I wake up and use it when I'm ready. I always include fruit, spinach, chia, or flaxseed for each bag, and sometimes add other items.

Assembling smoothies will be a quick process if you choose pre-cut frozen fruit. While putting together your smoothies, include local raw honey or organic maple syrup to add to the sweetness. Adding this, of course, is entirely optional, as fruit smoothies are already super sweet.

The final thing you should prepare during your monthly meal prep time will be your freezer meals—first, the more straightforward "assembly line" bags, and then the more involved freezer dishes. I haven't shouted as loudly about any of the different parts of your meal prep day, but HERE IS YOUR GAME CHANGER. Seriously! When you cook one of these meals for yourself or your family, making them with raw meat, the flavors can meld together during the thawing process, making for a delicious dish! Preparing raw freezer meals will afford you freshly cooked meals throughout the month. You will not cook them until the day you eat them, thus why they taste so fresh. When you discover for yourself what a game changer this type of meal is, you may load up more of these and cut back on other items. I wouldn't blame you!

If you are using any frozen meat, pull them out of the freezer about an hour or two before you'll need them. Doing so will allow them to thaw just enough to work with them, but not entirely. You need as much space cleared out and a spotless area, so you don't promote any bacteria growth while working with raw meat. Be sure to clean your site well and put away any items you have completed working with for this session.

Cut and prepare any veggies that you need for your freezer meals. Look ahead and cut, slice, dice, cube, mince absolutely every veggie and herb required for this big finale of your monthly meal prep, and set aside like items, so you can quickly grab them as you go down the assembly line of your freezer meal creations.

Plan to work with one type of meat at a time, so even if you have three different chicken meals, you can prepare them all together, but don't cross-contaminate beef cubes with chicken thighs, etc. Not only is this more sanitary to keep them separated (unless they're going into the same dish), but it also helps organize this part more easily and quickly.

Set up your bag racks, pull out your notecards of the freezer meals you are about to prepare, hook the appropriate pre-written gallon-sized bags to the bag racks and get ready to move through this section faster than you can imagine!

While your meat remains in the fridge until the last minute, put all the other ingredients needed into each bag. Set it up like an assembly line, and start down the row. For example, they all get salt; the first three get sliced green peppers; all six get sliced onions, etc., until all the ingredients are in the bag. Then add the meat. The beautiful thing about these bag racks is there is no touching these bags until your hands are clean. After adding the meat to each bag, wash your hands thoroughly and remove each one from the rack. Squeeze as much air out of each as you can, seal it, and lay it flat. Once you have all the like-meat freezer meals assembled and packed, place them flat into your freezer, stacked on top of each other. When you're sure to expel adequate air from them, you will be amazed at how many meals you can stack in a relatively small space.

The last freezer meals to attack will be those that are more involved; meat-loaves or maple bacon-wrapped pork loins. These are always completed last for two reasons. First, getting the quickest wins out of the way will make you feel accomplished. Second, because items that won't stack flat will just get in your way during the earlier processes, it's better to be able to stuff these more-rounded "rolls" of food wherever there is room.

Dear sister, YOU DID IT! I know you're exhausted, but what an accomplishment! You have enough food to last you and your family for an entire month! All you'll need to purchase between now and next month's prep will be fresh produce and other quick side items, should you run out. Of course, you may want to cook an additional meal or treat with all the extra time on your hands too! But NEEDING to cook was just solved in four hours, give or take. You have no excuse not to stick to your healthy lifestyle with a mountain of options!

"This is what the Lord of Heaven's Armies says: Be strong and finish the task" (Zechariah 8:9a)! My sweet sister, that is precisely what you've done! Zechariah was referring to building the Lord's Temple, and you just completed the creation of a month's worth of food that will properly and adequately nourish your temple! Your accomplishment is worthy of praise!

Chapter 8

S—STORAGE

Have them gather all the food produced in the good years that are just ahead and bring it to Pharaoh's storehouses. Store it away, and guard it so there will be food in the cities.

Genesis 41:35

Since the beginning of history, food has been stored away for the potential of hard seasons ahead. As Joseph recommends in Genesis of Pharaoh, knowing the famine was coming.

Can you philosophize that our hectic and time-constrained lives might be those hard seasons you need to store up to survive? Is it a far stretch? Consider what options you consume when you don't have meals ready at home. Were they always the healthiest possible options? If so, you are a rare one! This excellent exercise you just completed is the hard work you have done to build up your storehouses! Rejoice!

There is no universal method for food storage for everyone, so here are some of what works for me. In time, you will come up with the perfect system for you! But, and I can't stress enough, especially if you have extra freezer storage space available, you must have a strategy! Otherwise, items will be lost and forgotten.

First, cover what can remain in the refrigerator immediately after your meal prep session. The USDA recommends you consume all leftover items within four days, so keep out enough of what you plan to eat, of your cooked food, for that amount of time. Additionally, I have successfully kept my bagels without spoilage in my refrigerator for a week, but I must freeze some of my other bread types beyond a couple of days, or they will mold.

Once meal prep day has arrived, your freezer looks much different than it did the previous day, I'm sure! Before you begin, it doesn't hurt to do one more good sweep to be sure you've cleaned out anything no longer worth saving. Do this freezer check before you arrange your prepped meals and when you inventory before your next meal prep day. That's your priority. If you survey what is in your freezer for the first time doing this, I'll bet a large majority of what you find are items that have been in there way too long, are freezer burnt, or are foods you are going to stop consuming anyway. Do you know how long I kept the top layer of our wedding cake in our freezer? I'm embarrassed to elaborate. Let's just say it's gone now, and we never ate even a bite of the thing, and it took up quite a block of space.

Freeze individual portions (or no more than double portions) of any quick heat-up meals you have prepared. Items like chili, casseroles, etc., should all be kept in separate glass containers so you can heat up enough for a serving with enough left over for a second meal.

If you are freezing items that risk being stuck together, like egg bites or sausage balls, you don't have to place them in individual bags; unless you want them to be easy "grab and go" items to pack for work or school. I'll give you the secret that took me 45 years to learn! Once cooled from the oven, place the individual pieces on a pan lined with parchment paper in the freezer for an hour or two. Then, you can throw them all in the same bag and pull one or two out when you're ready.

Unless you are very disciplined, the only exception to individual bags is for sweet treats. Freeze your sweet treats in separate bags. I must do this, but you need to know your limits! If I reach into a bag of a dozen cookies, I may pull out 3 or 4. If I go into the freezer and grab one individually packaged, I'll be a "good girl" and stick to one. Again, if you are starting this new meal prep journey for a healthy lifestyle change, these are the things in which you have to be honest with yourself!

If you are freezing items you want to use for sandwiches, like bagels or hamburger buns, slice them before freezing them. Simply place a small piece of parchment paper between the slices, and they'll be easier to work with when you are ready to thaw and eat.

If you have a vacuum sealer, you can seal and preserve many solid items even longer in your freezer. However, only partially vacuum your fresh bread, as they don't bounce back after freezing. They'll still taste great, but they'll be (what I call) "mushed yumminess!"

Most raw freezer meals I make are in plastic gallon freezer bags and can be stacked flat on each other. If you fix enough to have two four-serving meals per week, that is just eight of those meals, and you can easily stack all eight of those on top of each other on one shelf in any size freezer.

I have my deep freezer divided into sections that I can list from right to left:

- Individually prepared meals
- Raw freezer meals & raw marinated meats
- Extra meat
- Veggies & fruit
- All meat bones/veggie scraps to make stock
- One separate rack for individual frozen desserts, homemade pumpkin puree, paw-paw pulp from our trees, etc.

If you are stacking foods in an upright freezer, you'll want to keep your extra meat on the bottom. You won't enjoy raw meat dripping onto your other foods in an emergency freezer thaw from a power outage, etc. Next, you should put your freezer meals on the rack above the unprepared meat and then all cooked items, fruits, and veggies above in the best order for your convenience.

If you have some foods in the freezer from a previous month still available, store them in the freezer up front and on top of the other similar meals to rotate through the oldest food first. Freezer meals will last for months, but you don't want to keep burying old ones and find "the great Chicken Fajitas of 2020" one day when it's 2022. I may or may not be speaking from experience!

Something to briefly note, too: if you want to take your family food prep to a whole other level, you may start raising your fresh organic veggies. As certain crops come in, you will want to allow extra freezer space and consider learning to can your produce. I raise a large garden and purposely grow enough tomatoes, peppers, and onions for homemade salsas, BBQ sauce, ketchup, etc. When I have a year with many beans, potatoes, or squash, I'll preserve them for future use by canning them. During apple season, I get a couple of bushels from our local farm and make a year's supply of apple butter, apple sauce, and spiced apples for the family to enjoy and share for Christmas gifts. Additional canned items like this can lend themselves to more accessible and budget-friendly monthly meal prep.

As I mentioned, extra freezer storage is "nice to have," and this is something I could write an entire chapter on alone. If you are thrifty like me, you will be free to stock up when prices are low. You will also find you can go bigger with your garden and bounty!

Also, consider the freedom for creativity having adequate freezer space gives you. I can prep my raw freezer meals once a quarter, making an even shorter monthly meal prep session two out of every three months. I can shop extra when there are sales. I can make extra sweet treats that freeze well and much more. You are likely thinking you don't have extra room for another appliance. I have lived in a 500-square-foot farmhouse in which the only option for a location would be a dorm-size freezer to double as a nightstand in the only bedroom. If it is a priority, you will find a place.

I have almost always had some sort of garage, outbuilding, or a separate room in the house where I could put a freezer. We currently live in a small three-bedroom ranch home built 70 years ago. We have a 2nd foyer in our home, where we have created our freezer and pantry space for canned items.

Again, you can get by without an additional freezer, but the possibilities become endless when you even have a little extra space for more prepared food.

In the long run, especially if you are purchasing inexpensive used freezers, you will ALWAYS get far more than your money's worth in the savings of groceries by being able to take advantage of sales or purchasing in bulk.

Are you living with limited space? Here's what one of my clients said about meal prepping in a small area:

> We currently live in a camper (my husband, grandson, and myself); learning how to meal prep has saved our lives. Living in this tiny cramped space while our house is being built makes eating very difficult, and if we had to plan daily what we were going to eat would have us reverting back to our old habits of eating quick junk for sure.
>
> —Jennifer C.

Jennifer brings up another excellent point about space. I am confident that all of these great ideas I give you to "just put it in your freezer" leave you wondering who has a freezer big enough for all of this. Take Jennifer's example of living in a camper as proof that anyone can do this.

The most crucial storage info that applies to meal preppers of all types concerns the storage of reheatable meals. Anything that you will be heating must always be in glass. Plastic zipper bags you will be dumping into a crockpot are fine, but I'm referring to anything you will be microwaving in the container. This purge was a tough transition for me, but there has been so much research proving how harmful it is to reheat in plastic. Yes, glass containers are more expensive than plastic, but unfortunately, it took cancer to come into my home to remind me that the three trash bags full of plastic I had been holding on to for years were not worth more than my family's health. Please make the transition if you haven't already.

Freezing with canning jars is possible too! Just be cautious if you are doing so, to give them at least 1½" headspace as the contents will expand. Canning jars will crack if they experience a rapid temperature change. You must let the jars cool before placing them in the freezer and give them time to thaw in the fridge or on the counter before heating them.

Oh, and don't forget about your stock that you have slow cooking for a few days! You will LOVE having this ingredient on hand whenever you cook rice and quinoa or make soups or other freezer meals next month. Of course, if you have a pressure canner, this is the best option for your stocks, and they'll last up to 18 months in your pantry, saving freezer space!

If you made some excellent dry ingredients to keep on hand, like pancake mix, seasoning blends, chili and taco mix, etc., keep those in a canning jar in your pantry well labeled with the date and name of what it is, plus any instructions, if necessary. For example, on the pancake mix, you may attach a label that says, "Pancake mix—12/5/22—Add 1/3 cup water to 1 cup mix." Most of these items will last an extended period, much like the spices and mixes you purchase from the store.

Finally, eat what you have, which should go without saying! But if you are entirely switching your lifestyle, this might take some adjustment. Eat your food! That's why it's there! Plus, you have options, so there's always something good to eat. Will you get whiny and be tempted sometimes? Sure. We all do, but that's the enemy tempting you. Once you get an excellent nourishing meal in your system, those thoughts will disappear, and you will be so proud of yourself for making the right decision!

"So whether you eat or drink, or whatever you do, do it all for the glory of God" (1 Corinthians 10:31). This verse should always be on the forefront of your mind when you take on a healthier lifestyle for the good of the temple you temporarily occupy! And give Him thanks and all the glory for the bounty you have created with His help.

Also, stick to your plan of eating out. If you only budgeted two meals out to eat for the month, stick to it! Yes, you'll have the occasional emergency that will dictate otherwise, but how about choosing a less expensive item, like a cup of hot tea at the local deli, instead of a full meal? Use your judgment, but try to hold as firm as possible to what you planned.

You will, unfortunately, have some people who simply won't understand your new lifestyle, and I've quickly learned that those who truly love me will be over the moon proud of what I'm doing. Those who aren't? Take a reminder from scripture: "Obviously, I'm not trying to win the approval of people, but of God. If pleasing people were my goal, I would not be Christ's servant" (Galatians: 1:10).

We can apply this to anything we do to draw closer to Him and prepare our temples to be healthier for His tasks. Always feel right about this, sister!

Chapter 9

YOUR FIRST 4-HOUR MEAL
PREP PLAN RECIPES

A ll of the following recipes show an example of everything I would make in one 4-hour session monthly. Each of these recipes make enough for 2 people for an entire month; however, if you are making these for just one person, you can still either make the same amount and have enough food for two months, as it will last, or cut the amounts in half.

For nutritional info about each recipe, full color pictures, and other recipes for foods mentioned in this book, download the eCookbook at :
Gift.SimplifyCleanEating.com or scan the QR code below

Breakfasts

Bacon & Gruyere Egg Muffins

Ingredients

10 Eggs

8 slices Bacon, Cooked (chopped)

1 cup Gruyere Cheese (shredded)

1 cup Baby Spinach (chopped)

¼ tsp Sea Salt

Directions

1. Preheat the oven to 400ºF (205ºC) and grease a muffin tray or use a silicone muffin tray.

2. In a large bowl, whisk the eggs. Add the remaining ingredients and stir to combine.

3. Portion the mixture into the muffin tray, filling each cup about 3/4 of the way full. Bake for 12 to 15 minutes, or until set. Cool for five minutes.

4. Makes 12 individual servings. Bag 1-2 servings separately and freeze up to 3 months. Thaw & reheat when ready.

Sausage Balls

Ingredients

3 lbs Pork Sausage

3 cups Almond Flour

3 cups Cheddar Cheese (shredded)

3 Egg

3/4 cup Parmigiano Reggiano (shredded)

1/4 cup Dried Onion Flakes

2 tbsps Baking Powder

Directions

1. Preheat the oven to 350 degrees.

2. Mix together and form into 1-1.5" balls and place on a baking sheet.

3. Bake for 20 minutes at 350 degrees.

4. Makes approximately 24 servings of 3 sausage balls each.

5. Meal prep option #1: Cook prior to freezing in bags with 1-2 servings per bag.

6. Meal prep option #2: Prepare raw sausage balls and freeze 24 in each of 3 aluminum pans with above cooking instructions written on lid.

Both options freeze well and give you the flexibility to choose if you want to cook them on your monthly meal prep day, or have them ready to cook when ready. Both options freeze well for up to 3 months.

Smoothies

Blueberry Flax Smoothie

Ingredients

6 cup Frozen Blueberries

12 cups Baby Spinach

1 ½ cups Whole Flax Seeds

6 cups Coconut Water

Directions

1. In 12 individual baggies fill each with ½ cup blueberries, ⅛ cup flax seeds, and 1 cup spinach.

2. Label baggies with name, date & instructions to add ½ cup coconut water and blend.

3. Freeze up to 3 months.

Chocolate Avocado Smoothie

Ingredients

3 Avocado

12 cup Baby Spinach

¾ cup Sunflower Seed Butter

12 scoops Collagen Powder (optional)

1 ½ cups Cocoa Powder

12 cup Coconut Milk

¼ cup Psyllium Husk Powder (optional)

Directions

1. In 12 individual baggies fill each with ¼ avocado, 2 tbsp cocoa powder, 1 tbsp sunflower seed butter, 1 cup spinach, and 1 scoop collagen & 1 tsp psyllium husk powders, if using.

2. Label baggies with name, date & instructions to add 1 cup coconut milk and blend.

3. Freeze up to 3 months.

Breads

Meal Prep Bagels

Ingredients

5 cups Mozzarella Cheese (shredded)	4 ozs Cream Cheese, Regular
4 Egg	3 cups Almond Flour
2 tsps Baking Powder	2 tbsps Everything Bagel Seasoning

Directions

1. Melt cheeses together in the microwave, one minute at a time, stirring in between. 2 minutes is usually sufficient.

2. Mix remaining ingredients together (Everything Bagel Seasoning can go on top of bagels or mixed in), then add the cheese in. Mixing with hands.

3. Separate into 12 equal size balls, pressing into the donut pan. Sprinkle top with seasoning, if not mixed in.

4. Bake at 400 degrees for 14 minutes.

5. Can be refrigerated for a week or frozen up to 3 months.

6. Freezing option #1: Slice fresh bagel, place halves on cookie sheet and set in freezer for 1-2 hours, then put whole bagels in baggies in freezer.

7. Freezing option #2: Slice fresh bagel, place parchment paper in between slices and freeze individual bagels in baggie.

Snacks

Pecan Trail Mix

Ingredients

6 cup Pecans

1 ½ cups Pumpkin Seeds

1 ½ cups Dried Unsweetened Cranberries   12 oz Dark Chocolate Chunks

Directions

1. Add all of the ingredients into a large bag. Mix together well.
2. Divide into individual snack baggies with 24 half-cup servings, or keep in large zipper bags or jars in pantry.

Toasted Quinoa Energy Bites

Ingredients

3/4 cup Quinoa (uncooked)

2 cups Quick Oats

2/3 cup Unsweetened Shredded Coconut

1/2 cup Cacao Nibs

3/4 cup Sunflower Seed Butter (unsweetened)

1/3 cup Raw Honey

Directions

1. Toast quinoa in saucepan on medium heat for about 5-10 minutes or until it's popping & browned.
2. Pulse oats in a food processor or blender briefly to make them more fine.
3. Place all ingredients in a medium mixing bowl & mix well.
4. Use a medium sized scoop, or hands, to make tightly formed balls and place on parchment paper on a large sheet pan.
5. Place in the freezer on pan for 2 hours, then store in plastic baggies for up to 3 months.

Peanut Butter Mocha Chia Pudding

Ingredients

10 ½ cups Coconut Milk

¾ cups Cacao Powder

¾ cup All Natural Peanut Butter

1 ½ tsp Stevia Powder (to taste)

3 cups Coffee (brewed drip or espresso)

2 cups Chia Seeds

12 scoops Collagen Powder (optional)

Directions

1. Add all ingredients to a blender and blend for at least one minute, until completely smooth. Scoop into bowls of 1-2 servings and freeze up to 3 months. This recipe makes 24 servings.

2. Thaw overnight in refrigerator before eating.

*Note, if you have a smaller blender, you may need to cut all ingredients in half and make half a batch at a time.

Main Dish Meals

Classic Meatloaf Freezer Meal

Ingredients

6 Egg

1 ½ Yellow Onion (peeled, finely chopped)

3 tbsp Coconut Aminos

1 ½ cup Oats

1 ½-2lbs bacon (optional)

1 cup Tomato Paste

1 lb Mushrooms (finely chopped)

1 tbsp Sea Salt

4 ½ lbs Lean Ground Beef

Directions

1. Mix all ingredients together, except bacon, and form into 3 loaves.

2. Wrap each in bacon, if desired.

3. Place each in separate gallon freezer bags labeled with date and instructions stating to place in slow cooker on low for 6-8 hours.

4. Freeze up to 3 months and thaw overnight prior to cooking.

Hawaiian Chicken Kabobs Freezer Meal

Ingredients

6 lbs Chicken Breast (bite-sized pieces)   ⅓ cup Coconut Aminos

¾ cup Apple Cider Vinegar   1 bulb Garlic (minced)

6 Lime (juiced)   ⅓ cup Ginger (peeled and grated)

1 tbsp Cayenne Pepper   6 Green Bell Pepper (large chunks)

6 Yellow Bell Pepper (large chunks)   6 cups Cherry Tomatoes

12 cups Pineapple (large chunks)   6 cups Red Onion (large chunks)

Directions

1. Create marinade by combining coconut aminos, apple cider vinegar, garlic, lime juice, ginger and cayenne pepper in a bowl. Stir well.

2. Freezer Meal option #1: Assemble skewers by alternating raw chicken, peppers, onion, tomatoes, and pineapple. Divide between 3 labeled gallon freezer bags and pour divided marinade over each. Store flat in freezer up to 3 months. Thaw when ready to grill. Grill for approximately 15 minutes or until chicken cooked through.

3. Time-Saving Freezer Meal option #2: Don't assemble skewers, simply place the raw chicken, peppers, onion, tomatoes, and pineapple divided between 3 labeled gallon freezer bags. Divide marinade and pour over each. Store flat in freezer up to 3 months. Thaw when ready to grill. Cook these in a grill basket, or sauté on your stove top in a skillet.

Easy Chicken Fajitas Freezer Meal

Ingredients

½ cup Avocado Oil

¼ cup Chili Powder

2 tsp Sea Salt

4 Yellow Bell Pepper (sliced)

3 ½ lb Chicken Breast (strips)

⅛ cup Cumin

4 Green Bell Pepper (sliced)

4 Yellow Onion (sliced)

32 Corn Tortilla (don't need on meal prep day)

Directions

1. Put all ingredients, except tortillas, divided between 4 gallon zipper bags, dated and labeled with instructions stating to place in a slow cooker, cook 4 hrs and serve on tortillas with toppings of choice.

2. Store flat in freezer up to 3 months.

Slow Cooker Beef Stew Freezer Meal

Ingredients

⅓ cup Extra Virgin Olive Oil

¾ cup Red Wine Vinegar

3 Sweet Onion (diced)

3 cup Beef Broth

1 tbsp Sea Salt

6 lbs Stewing Beef (bite-size pieces)

6 cups Baby Carrots

7 ½ cups Mushrooms (sliced)

½ tbsp Dried Thyme

½ tbsp Black Pepper

3/4 cup Brown Rice Flour (don't need on meal prep day)

Directions

1. Divide all ingredients, except brown rice flour, among 3 dated and labeled gallon zipper freezer bags. Label should indicate to slow

cook 4-6 hours. Once beef cooked through, stir in ¼ cup brown rice flour, until liquid thickens.

2. Freeze in flattened bags up to 3 months. Thaw overnight before slow cooking.

Black Bean & Beef Chili

Ingredients

1/4 cup Avocado Oil	6 lbs Extra Lean Ground Beef
6 Yellow Onion (chopped)	4 Jalapeno Pepper (finely chopped)
16 Garlic (large cloves, minced)	1 cup Taco Seasoning
1/4 cup Cocoa Powder	1 cup Tomato Paste
16 cups Black Beans (cooked, rinsed well)	6 cups Diced Tomatoes
8 cups Vegetable Broth	Sea Salt & Black Pepper (to taste)

Directions

1. Heat the oil and ground beef in a large pot over medium heat until meat is browned. Add the onions and jalapeno and cook for about five minutes or until the onion begins to soften. Stir in the garlic, taco seasoning, and cocoa powder, and cook for another minute.

2. Add the tomato paste and black beans and mix well to combine, then add the diced tomatoes and vegetable broth. Season with salt and pepper to taste.

3. Bring the chili to a gentle boil then reduce the heat slightly and simmer for 15 to 20 minutes or until the chili has thickened.

4. Season with additional salt and pepper, if needed.

5. Freeze individual or double servings up to 3 months. This recipe makes 24 servings.

Maple Bacon Wrapped Pork Loin Freezer Meal

Ingredients

3 - 2 lbs Pork Tenderloins	1 ½ lbs Bacon
1 ½ cup Maple Syrup (organic)	½ cup Dijon Mustard (or spicy brown)
⅓ cup Apple Cider Vinegar (raw, organic)	3 tbsp Coconut Aminos
1 ½ tbsp Garlic (minced)	⅛ cup Black Pepper

Directions

1. Label 3 gallon size freezer bags with name of recipe, date and cooking instructions.
2. Pour maple syrup, mustard, vinegar, garlic, coconut aminos and pepper into a bowl and gently whisk to combine; set aside.
3. Begin at one end of each pork loin and tightly wrap bacon strips around continuing to the other end. Place each carefully in a dated and labeled gallon zipper freezer bag. Instructions on each bag should indicate to cook in slow cooker on low 7-8 hours.
4. Pour sauce divided over pork loins in all 3 bags. Press air from the bag and seal. Place in freezer up to 3 months.
5. When ready to cook, thaw in fridge overnight. When placed in slow cooker, squeeze marinade out of bag to cover pork loin.

Chili/Taco Seasoning

Ingredients

2 tbsps Black Pepper

2 tbsps Cayenne Pepper

1/4 cup Coriander

1/4 cup Sea Salt

1/4 cup Oregano

1/4 cup Garlic Powder (or granulated)

1/4 cup Onion Powder

1/2 cup Paprika

3/4 cup Cumin

1 1/2 cups Chili Powder

Directions

1. Mix all together in a container. Store in jar in pantry to use as needed.

If you're using this in a recipe telling you to use a packet of taco or chili seasoning, use ¼ cup of this mix.

GROCERY LIST FOR ABOVE ITEMS (SCALED FOR TWO PEOPLE)

Non-Perishable

6 cups Almond Flour

½ cup Cacao Nibs

12 oz Dark Chocolate

1 ½ cups Sunflower Seed Butter

1 ⅓ cup Maple Syrup

3 tbsp Cayenne Pepper

1 ¾ cups Chili Powder

1 cup Cumin

⅛ cup Everything Bagel Seasoning

¼ cup Garlic Powder

¼ cup Oregano

6 cups Pecans

½ cup Sea Salt

3 cups Beef Broth

16 cups Black Beans

4 14.5oz cans Diced Tomatoes

3 ½ cups Oats

1 cup Apple Cider Vinegar

¾ cup Coconut Aminos

⅓ cup Extra Virgin Olive Oil

8 ¼ oz Collagen Powder (optional)

⅓ cup Raw Honey

½ tbsp Stevia Powder

3 tbsp Baking Powder

2 ½ cups Cacao or Cocoa Powder

¾ cup Peanut Butter

3 cups Coffee (brewed)

⅓ cup Black Pepper

2 cups Chia Seeds

¼ cup Coriander

¼ cup Dried Onion Flakes

½ tbsp Dried Thyme

¼ cup Onion Powder

½ cup Paprika

1 ½ cups Pumpkin Seeds

1 ½ cups Whole Flax Seeds

8 cups Vegetable Broth

10 ½ cups Coconut Milk

3 6oz cans Tomato Paste

¾ cup Quinoa

¾ cup Avocado Oil

½ cup Dijon Mustard

¾ cup Red Wine Vinegar

1 ½ cups Dried Unsweet Cranberries

¼ cup Psyllium Husk Powder (optional)

⅔ cup Unsweetened Coconut Flakes

Perishable Items

3 Avocado	6 Lime
12 cups Pineapple	6 cups Frozen Blueberries
6 cups Baby Carrots	25 cups Baby Spinach
6 cups Cherry Tomatoes	2 ½ lb Mushrooms
3 Garlic Bulbs	⅓ cup Ginger
10 Green Bell Peppers	10 Yellow Bell Peppers
4 Jalapeño Peppers	15 Sweet/Yellow Onions
6 Red Onions	4 oz Cream Cheese
23 Eggs	1 cup Gruyere Cheese (or choice)
3 cups Cheddar Cheese	5 cups Mozzarella Cheese
¾ cups Parmigiano Reggiano	3-4 pounds sliced Bacon
9 ½ lbs Chicken Breast	10 ½ lbs Ground Beef
6 lbs Stewing Beef	3 lbs Ground Sausage
3 2-lbs Pork Tenderloin	

Items needed during month, but NOT on Meal Prep Day

6 cups Coconut Water	12 cups Coconut Milk
¾ cup Brown Rice Flour	32 Corn Tortillas
Toppings of choice for Fajitas	6 "steam bags" of veggies
Additional fresh fruit/veggies, if desired/needed	

Money Savings Tips for Sample Recipes

1. *Choose either Peanut Butter or Sunflower Seed Butter.*

2. *Choose either Raw Honey or Organic Maple Syrup.*

3. *Other than spices to make the Chili Seasoning, feel free to use what you have at home! Look at spices in these recipes as suggestions!*

4. *Start making your own Beef, Veggie and other broths/stocks. In the eCookbook, you will see instructions how to do this,*

5. *Dried beans are always going to cost less. 1 pound dried black beans = 6 cups soaked black beans. So for the 16 cups black beans needed for the chili, soak 2.5-3 pounds dry black beans overnight.*

6. *Collagen Powder & Psyllium Husk Powder are both optional for the smoothies. Feel free to skip those ingredients. They are good sources of protein & fiber when needed, but do not change the taste or consistency of those recipes.*

7. *No natural Stevia powder at home? Substitute with Monkfruit, Coconut Sugar or Organic Cane Sugar.*

8. *No Brown Rice Flour? Substitute Gluten Free All Purpose Flour Blend, Buckwheat Flour, Quinoa Flour, Chickpea or Garbanzo Bean Flour. You can also make your own at a much lower price by grinding organic brown rice in your blender until powdered.*

9. *Are yellow bell peppers a lot more expensive than green? Use all green!*

10. *No Gruyere Cheese, or too expensive? Choose any other!*

11. *Use Boneless Chicken Thighs instead of Breasts.*

12. *Use plain water instead of Coconut Water in Smoothies.*

ACTUAL STEP-BY-STEP PLAN

U se the checklists found at Resources.SimplifyCleanEating.com ("printable checklists") to make this plan even easier for all Inventory, Harvest, and Execute recommendations. This plan below, though, will show exactly how I would complete the previous 15 recipes in one 4-hour monthly meal prep session on meal prep day. This assumes you are already starting in a clean kitchen with staging area ready.

If you'd like printable 3x5 card info and bag labels for these exact recipes, rather than needing to write them all during your pre-work time the night before your meal prep day, you can get them here: Resources.SimplifyCleanEating.com

They all print on Avery Waterproof Labels #5264.

- Night before soak black beans (if using dry) for chili in water in large pot, and pull ground beef, sausage and bacon out of freezer, if frozen, and put in refrigerator.
- Day of: In non-staging area gather the following:
  a. 3x5 cards in following order:
     i. Chili Seasoning
     ii. Chili
     iii. Trail Mix
     iv. Egg Muffins
     v. Bagels

    vi. Sausage Balls

   vii. Quinoa Energy Bites

  viii. Chia Pudding

   ix. Chocolate Avocado Smoothie

    x. Blueberry Smoothie

   xi. Chicken Fajitas

   xii. Chicken Kabobs

  xiii. Beef Stew

  xiv. Meatloaf

   xv. Maple Bacon Pork Loin

b. Large mixing bowls

c. Canning funnel

d. Large pot

e. Skillet

f. Saucepan

g. Blender

h. Pre-labeled zipper bags

i. Jars & glass freezer containers

j. Muffin pan

k. Donut pan

l. Large Cookie Sheet

m. 3 Aluminum pans, if freezing raw sausage balls

n. Baggie racks

o. All non-perishable items purchased from shopping list

p. Avocados, Limes, Carrots, Cherry Tomatoes, mushrooms, garlic, ginger, peppers, onions

- Organize remaining cold/frozen fruits, vegetables, and meats so they are easily accessible in the refrigerator or freezer when you need them.
- Move large mixing bowl, canning funnel, large storage jar, and all ingredients for Chili Seasoning to staging area.
- Mix all ingredients and put in storage jar. Set storage jar aside, as you will use chili seasoning in two recipes during this session.
- Put ingredients away coriander, oregano, garlic & onion powders, and paprika.
- Put other ingredients back in storing area.
- Gather ingredients for chili and make in large pot on top of stove as indicated on recipe. Only cut veggies needed for chili at this time. (Once chili has completed cooking, you can turn on warm and keep covered for this evening's meal, and store away individual servings when ready.)
- Put avocado oil & chili seasoning back in storing area.
- Clean staging area.
- Gather large zipper bag and ingredients for Trail mix. Mix all together and store away in pantry in large bag. Will last all month in this bag, or you can choose to make individual ½ cup individual serving bags. For a time saver, I will keep it in the large bag that I mix it in.
- Put any ingredients away, if you have any remaining, from trail mix.
- Gather muffin pan and ingredients for Egg Muffins.
- Preheat oven to 400 degrees.
- Cook 8 slices chopped bacon on stove top in skillet & drain.
- Prepare Egg Muffins as indicated in recipe, and bake.
- Clean staging area.
- Gather donut pan and ingredients for bagels.

- Prepare bagels as indicated in recipe and put in oven as egg muffins come out.
- Put away Everything Bagel Seasoning.
- Brew coffee (feel free to drink some, but save 3 cups for chia pudding.)
- Keep Almond flour and baking powder at staging area and gather remaining ingredients for sausage balls, a large mixing bowl, and three aluminum pans (if freezing them in raw batches, which I am for this example.)
- Make sausage balls and place 24 formed balls in each of the 3 aluminum pans. Cover them with foil or matching aluminum lid for pan labeled with cooking instructions & date.
- Place raw sausage balls in freezer.
- Put cold ingredients back in refrigerator, and put away almond flour, baking powder and dried onion flakes.
- Clean staging area.
- If meat being used in main dish meals is frozen, pull out to start to thaw, and keep near storing area. We don't want this meat to fully thaw, just enough to work with.
- Gather large cookie sheet and ingredients for Quinoa Energy Bites.
- Start cooking quinoa on stovetop as indicated in recipe.
- Follow remaining recipe instructions and then place quinoa energy bites spread apart on cookie sheet in freezer for 1-2 hours minimum so they won't stick together when placed in freezer bag(s).
- Put the oats and sunflower seed butter back in storing area, and the rest of the ingredients away.
- Gather ingredients for chia pudding, including brewed coffee, and put blender in convenient location to use.
- Make chia pudding as indicated on recipe, and pour/scoop into individual glass freezer bowls. Put all in freezer as they are made.

If you intend to eat some in the first week, feel free to keep some in refrigerator.

- Put coconut milk, chia seeds, peanut butter and stevia away.
- Keep cacao/cocoa powder & collagen in staging areas.
- Gather 12 baggie racks, prelabeled baggies & remaining ingredients for Chocolate Avocado smoothies.
- Clip baggies on baggie racks.
- Cut avocados open & put ¼ avocado in each bag. Follow by all remaining ingredients in each bag.
- Seal all bags and place in freezer.
- Put sunflower seed butter, cocoa powder, collagen and psyllium husk powders away.
- Keep spinach in staging area.
- Gather the baggies, blueberries and flax seeds for blueberry smoothies.
- Clip baggies on baggie racks.
- Fill each bag as indicated in recipe. Seal all bags and place in freezer.
- Put all ingredients and 5 of the 12 baggie racks away.
- Clean staging area.
- Gather bags and all ingredients for the Chicken Fajita and Chicken Kabob recipes.
- Clip the bags on the remaining 7 baggie racks.
- Cut all onions and peppers for both recipes and place in bags as indicated (following easy freezer meal option for kabob recipe.)
- Add all remaining ingredients in each bag for both recipes as indicated.
- Cut all chicken, and add to bags.
- Wash hands and then seal all bags, squeezing as much air out of each, and laying flat in freezer stacked on top of each other.

- Put chili seasoning & 4 of the remaining 7 baggie racks away.
- Clean staging area.
- Gather ingredients (including all mushrooms) and pre-labeled bags for Beef Stew recipe.
- Cut all mushrooms and onions for beef stew and meatloaf recipes, and set aside 1 lb mushrooms and 1 ½ onions for meatloaf.
- Clip pre-labeled beef stew bags on baggie racks.
- Add all non-meat ingredients for beef stew to three bags.
- Add beef cubes to bags.
- Wash hands and then seal each bag, squeezing as much air out as possible.
- Place bags stacked flat in freezer.
- Put away all olive oil, red wine vinegar, broth and thyme.
- Put black pepper back in storing area.
- Clean staging area.
- Gather large mixing bowl, remaining ingredients, and pre-labeled bags for meatloaf.
- Clip pre-labeled meatloaf bags on baggie racks.
- Mix all ingredients, except bacon, in large mixing bowl for all 3 meatloaves.
- Follow recipe, and place carefully in each bag.
- Wash hands, seal each bag squeezing as much air out of each. Roll bag around each meatloaf and place in freezer.
- Put away oats & salt.
- Clean staging area.
- Gather all remaining ingredients and last pre-labeled bags.
- Clip pre-labeled pork loin bags on baggie racks.
- Mix marinade as indicated in recipe.

- Wrap each pork loin in bacon and place carefully in each bag.
- Wash hands.
- Pour an even amount of marinade over each.
- Seal each bag squeezing as much air out of each. Roll bag around each pork loin and place in freezer.
- Put all remaining ingredients away and clean kitchen!
- YOU DID IT!!!!

Sample one week meal plan using above recipes:

Sample Week
7 days

	Mon	Tue	Wed	Thu	Fri	Sat	Sun
Breakfast	February Blueberry Flax Smoothie	February Chocolate Avocado Smoothie	Bacon & Gruyere Egg Muffins	Sausage Balls	Sausage Balls	Bacon & Gruyere Egg Muffins	Bacon & Gruyere Egg Muffins
Snack 1	Toasted Quinoa Energy Bites	Peanut Butter Mocha Chia Pudding	Peanut Butter Mocha Chia Pudding	Pecan Trail Mix	Toasted Quinoa Energy Bites	Red Bell Pepper & Cheese	2 Prosciutto Wrapped Avocado
Lunch	Black Bean & Beef Chili	Classic Meatloaf Freezer Meal	Meal Prep Bagels	Easy Chicken Fajitas Freezer Meal	Maple Bacon Wrapped Pork Loin Freezer Meal	Black Bean & Beef Chili	Hawaiian Chicken Kabobs Freezer Meal
		Steamed Broccoli	Turkey, Greens & Avocado Wraps	Cucumber & Avocado Salad	Green Beans & Cauliflower Rice		0.5 Quinoa
Dinner	Classic Meatloaf Freezer Meal	Classic Meatloaf Freezer Meal	Easy Chicken Fajitas Freezer Meal	Maple Bacon Wrapped Pork Loin Freezer Meal	Maple Bacon Wrapped Pork Loin Freezer Meal	Hawaiian Chicken Kabobs Freezer Meal	Hawaiian Chicken Kabobs Freezer Meal
	Steamed Broccoli	Steamed Broccoli	Cucumber & Avocado Salad	Green Beans & Cauliflower Rice	Green Beans & Cauliflower Rice	0.5 Quinoa	0.5 Quinoa

This above meal plan is an example of how I would use these recipes in a week. I share multiple times throughout the book that one thing you gain in this lifestyle is the flexibility and freedom to have so many foods on hand that you can grab whatever you are in the mood for, or what works for your schedule that day.

Note that there are some side dishes listed and some other snacks of veggies, etc. This just shows how you can add in some additional items, as needed and desired. Also, where words are grayed out, this indicates having leftovers on hand from cooking one of the raw freezer meals. (My meal plan program which I use allows me to choose a number of servings, which is why "2" and "0.5" are noted in some places.)

Chapter 10

CONCLUSION

*And people should eat and drink and enjoy the fruits
of their labor, for these are gifts from God.*

Ecclesiastes 3:13

Sweet sister, you have labored and have accomplished so much for which you should be proud! Even though the actual four to six-ish hour period may not have been the most fun you have ever experienced, can you believe you just provided yourself an easy way to consume all healthy meals and even snacks for thirty days? This exercise takes no time, considering the impact you just had on your and your family's health!

Just to recap my Monthly Meal Prep system:

- **R**—you now **REALIZE** the importance of a healthy lifestyle and how this fantastic tool of Monthly Meal Prep is a game changer to your health, wealth & time.

- **I**—you have **INVENTORIED** your pantry and freezer and **IDEN- TIFIED** your plan for meal prep for the month.

- **C**—you have scheduled your Monthly Meal Prep day for this coming month on your **CALENDAR** and are holding it sacred. You may have involved a friend in this, too.

- **H**—you have **HARVESTED** all of your Monthly Meal Prep supplies and ingredients, and if it matters to you, have done so in a budget-friendly way.
- **E**—you have **EXECUTED** your Monthly Meal Prep.
- **S**—you have **STORED** all your bounties and will eat healthy, clean meals for an entire month with little to no additional effort!

I want to congratulate you for taking this extraordinary, life-changing step. Once you get in the groove of this system after a month or two, learn your favorite recipes to rotate so you aren't too repetitive and physically feel the time gained, improved health, and money savings; you will never look back!

I hope that you are feeling equipped and inspired, and I'd love to share some of my favorite recipes to get you started, which I mention throughout the book. Just visit Gift.SimplifyCleanEating.com or scan the QR code below.

Don't miss out on these extra 50 recipes!

If you'd like to discover a world of improved health, be sure to continue reading the last few pages of this book! Though, if you *never* need my hand-holding because I have provided everything here, I am thrilled to have given you what you need! However, you can follow me on social media, as I'm always sharing new recipes and tips about living a healthy, toxin-free lifestyle. I also send out "Massey's Monday Meal" weekly to my email subscribers! Again, check out my website for many ways to stay connected!

Sister, stay in touch and let me know just how much your health and life have improved through these changes you are making. I love to give God the glory for His healed lives through what I teach. I know you are going to be no different! And then, all I ask is that you share this message! Tell everyone! You now have a cure (or at least a massive improvement) for so much of what physically ails our world. Don't keep this a secret!

Go to the Temple and give the people this message of life!

Acts 5:20

God Bless!
Wendy

CLIENT MEAL PREP TESTIMONIALS

Wendy's approach helped us to save money by eating out much less and got us back in the kitchen, working together, which also continued to bless our marriage.

—Ted K., Herndon, VA

Meal prepping has helped me succeed with the program. I have to say that if I do not meal prep, I do not do as well with my eating and keeping with my goals. Wendy's videos that she offers on meal prepping have been a wealth of information, and I learn something new all the time.

—Shelley B., Moseley, VA

In the past couple of weeks, I have already been much better with meal prepping. Having things on hand has helped me make a lifestyle change because we all like convenience when it comes to busy weekdays. It's funny because you think you'd be spending more money, but I have noticed we have been able to save a ton of money because we are mainly eating at home, and a little bit at the grocery store can go a long way. It has saved us time also, especially on busy days.

—Brittany G., Taneytown, MD

Wendy stressed that meal prep was going to help, and it did tremendously. There's no guessing what I'm having for any meal, and it helped me determine how to prepare it so that I could eat it during the week.

Meal prep is so key. It keeps me from straying because my meals and snacks are ready to go.

—Aaron S., Odenton, MD

While it appears that meal prepping takes up too much time overall, it actually saves time in the long run. Rather than being hungry "in the moment" and resorting to unhealthy options, meal prepping is a reliable plan to help you stay on course throughout the week.

—Amy F., Glen Allen, VA

HOW I CAN HELP YOU BEYOND THIS BOOK

T hank you for devoting your time to reading this message, about which I'm so passionate! I also want to make you aware of some other options I offer to those who would like additional support if you don't want to go on this journey alone. Plus, if you do not want to read labels to find the healthiest clean foods, have any desire to search for the best meat options or if the thought of comparison shopping sounds like no fun, then allow me to plug my Monthly Meal Prep Club.

I have a 4-Hour Monthly Meal Prep Club, which is a subscription service, in which I provide many items to make this process even quicker and smoother for you:

- Recipes for upcoming month's meal prep.
- Printable shopping list.
- Printable "3x5 card" info.
- Easy, quick shopping links for "Wendy-approved foods."
- Budget-conscious recipes.
- Fun monthly themed "Prep With Me" webinar. (Video replay available to all club members.)
- Monthly prizes awarded.

When I polled my social media friends and asked what stopped them from meal prepping, the first concern was time, and the second one was that it was all too overwhelming. That is why I created my club subscription and strive to improve your experience.

If you would like more info on how to join, please go to www.MasseyWellnes.com/members

Please visit my website for information about scheduling a free consultation to discuss my coaching programs, which have helped change many lives. I have extended programs that empower folks to gain control over their health. They assist those losing their quality of life due to disease, excessive weight, and prescriptions. They improve energy and sleep, reduce or eliminate pharmaceutical dependency, and aid in loving their reflection in the mirror.

I have helped so many people improve countless disease processes with nutrition alone. It's true! Conditions like high blood pressure, diabetes, chronic hypoglycemia, high cholesterol, thyroid disorders, chronic gastrointestinal disorders such as IBS, GERD, chronic colitis, etc. chronic pain and migraines, seizure disorders, chronic asthma, rheumatoid and psoriatic arthritis, chronic acne & eczema, other inflammatory conditions, sleep apnea, miserable menopausal symptoms—like severe hot flashes, and so many more controllable diseases through proper nutrition!

Both this lifestyle and monthly meal prep are game changers!

ACKNOWLEDGMENTS

I would like to thank one of my pastors, Mike Palmer. I don't know that he realizes the immense impact of his messages on Sundays, his smiles and hugs in between services, and his one-on-one inspirational discussions and "real talk" have been to me. Your message in early 2022 reminded me that my plans aren't necessarily God's plans and that His could be much bigger than my brain could fathom. When I shared my vision for taking my health message and turning it into a ministry, you mentioned writing a book would be a great way to do this, and I laughed. Well, you planted the seed, and God took it from there. He didn't think it was a laughing matter at all! Thank you from the bottom of my heart!

To my sister, Amity, not only has your health improvement been a significant catalyst for the fire that fuels Massey Wellness, but I can't thank you enough for how much you played a part in this project. When I had this opportunity, you saw the big picture and realized my potential that I didn't even see in myself. I don't know that I would have taken this huge step to complete this work if you didn't encourage me to. Thank you also for your editing help, as you are one of the most intelligent people I know!

To my Daddy in heaven, your love and support of me in everything I do was something so many little girls and grown women never experience. Thank you from the bottom of my heart, and I just know you're looking down on me and smiling—and knowing you—the happy tears are flowing.

To my Mommy. Though you likely won't get the opportunity to read this— Perhaps you will—Please know that you are one of my greatest motivators for getting this message out! Dementia is a horrible condition, and I want to help as many people prevent having to watch those they love to experience such torment. I love you so much!

To my Lifepoint "small group" ladies: Sarah, Angi, Rebecca, Lisa, Lisa, Malerie, Deanna, Liz, Joan, and Linda. The prayers, excitement, love, and encouragement you all have shown me throughout this process have been so appreciated! Thursday mornings with you all each week make my world complete! And Sarah, some of your prayers for my protection from the enemy during this process have been profound. I've meditated on your words interceding on my behalf many a moment.

To my business mentor, Nicole, I would still be scrambling, trying to figure out what to do with all the data I had in my brain that I needed to get out. I would still be aching to find a way to help others, and you helped make that a reality. Thank you!

To Donna Partow, my author/publishing mentor, to have this opportunity to work with you has been something I would have never dreamed of when I discovered your book that tearful day at a truck stop in Tennessee. Not only have you been a spiritual light in my life, but to have God bring us together for this project is still evidence of the neverending provision of our Heavenly Father. I am so proud to be in the same Family as you, and I can't thank you enough for your expertise and this experience.

To my "WendySquared," you are always a bright light in a dark room and always the one who can help remove the fog so I can see the blue sky. Thank you for your prayers, love, and encouragement.

To Carrie. Your editing expertise was priceless. I could never possibly repay you!

To my many clients, but—in particular—Joy. Not to leave any others out who have been incredibly supportive, but the support you have shown me throughout this journey has been immeasurable. You have trusted new strategies I want to try and prayed for me. You have been a large part of my motivation for many days to keep plugging forward. I love you! You're such an extraordinary woman, and you genuinely do F.R.O.G!

To Aaron. Watching your health improve and how you continue to wow the world with your activity level overflows my heart. This is why I do this.

To Tony and Gina. Something about the bond we've built is unique, and I can't thank you enough for being my prayer warriors and sounding board for my ideas throughout this evolution.

To Margie. John 15:13. I love you so much!

To Swing, my grill master. The unconditional love, listening ear, and support of everything I do is something I always appreciate!

To the many people who have encouraged me, asked me to write books, asked me to create cookbooks and resources, and requested so many things I try to provide—thank you for seeing the value I have to share. I never dreamed when I went to nursing school that the turn of events that occurred just eight years later would lead me down such a path. God is incredible, and I am so humbled.

ABOUT THE AUTHOR

Wendy Massey is a wife, mom of three, GiGi, nurse, holistic nutrition specialist, student, coach, servant, and child of the One Living God. She has a deep love for cooking, gardening, homesteading and live music, which brought her and her husband, Bill, together.

Wendy has worked in the nursing field since age 19 (1993) when she became a Certified Nursing Assistant. She then obtained her Registered Nurse license in 2005 through Southside Regional Medical Center and Richard Bland College in Petersburg, Va. She worked most of her career as an Emergency and Trauma RN and was, at one time, one of only 1500 nurses in the country who had earned both prestigious emergency certifications (CEN & CPEN).

She returned to school to obtain her Bachelors in Holistic Health Sciences through a small international holistic-focused university (IQUIM) in Honolulu, HI, and has continued her studies with them in pursuit of her Ph.D. in Integrative Medicine. She expects to graduate in 2024.

Wendy's passion for health is infectious. Every day she follows her calling to help people remove the unhealthy veil that covers so many eyes so they can see the power they have to heal themselves of so much of what ails them by utilizing proper nutrition. She's cheerful and always full of love, but she has such a burden on her heart to shed light where there is so much darkness causing people to become unnecessarily diseased. She hopes to inspire many with this book and her public influence so that she can help God's Kingdom be vital for the tasks they are called to while in their temporary home.

A NOTE TO YOU, THE READER:

I want to encourage you to improve your life. You certainly don't have to make every change I recommend to realize improved health, though if you keep making small changes, the impact will be tremendous!

I hope I've provided you with some motivation or a respite from the day-to-day challenges you may be dealing with.

COULD YOU PLEASE DO ME A SMALL FAVOR?

I put my heart and soul into my education, helping others heal with nutrition and finding more straightforward ways to do so. I spent hundreds of hours writing this book, edited it six times (with plenty of help), got the cover just right, plus a bunch of other behind-the-scenes stuff. It's been a massive project that's taken me years to complete. This book means a lot to me as it's my way to reach out to help, motivate, and inspire greatness and health improvement in you and other readers.

Please take a moment right now to leave your heartfelt comments on Amazon. Your review will help someone who hasn't read the book yet know what you liked about it and why they should take their time to read it. I love getting honest feedback and will read every single review, including yours. Reviews make a HUGE difference to authors—Writing a review is the very best way to help me out :)

To post your review, please visit: Review.SimplifyCleanEating.com

Made in the USA
Middletown, DE
27 December 2023

46825029R00071